RETIRING WELL

Retiring WELL

HOW TO ENJOY RETIREMENT IN **ANY** ECONOMY

Michael Reese, CFP®

HOST OF THE TV SHOW *RETIRING WELL WITH MICHAEL REESE, CFP®*

LIONCREST
PUBLISHING

RETIRING WELL

How to Enjoy Retirement in Any Economy

ISBN   978-1-61961-888-6 *Paperback*

978-1-61961-889-3 *Ebook*

To my loving wife, Becky, for her support in every area of life. I would be lost without you.

Contents

SECTION I

═══

Investment
Plan

CHAPTER 1

John and Sara

Meet John and Sara. Good people. John enlisted in the Army straight out of high school. After serving his country, he came home and went to college. This is where he met Sara, in English class. She was the cute girl in the fourth row with a smile that melted his heart. After working up his courage, he asked her out to dinner, and to his surprise, she said yes.

The two of them hit it off right away, and soon they were dating regularly. Almost immediately after college, the engagement was on and they were married.

John got a job in sales with IBM. Sara became a schoolteacher, third grade. Two years into marriage, along came their first child, Steven. Following Steven was Jennifer, and finally little James. John and Sara were happy—your typical white-picket-fence family with a house full of healthy children and a Golden Retriever named Comet.

You can see them in your mind's eye, can't you?

Like many couples with small children, they started saving for college, and of course, their retirement. Early on, they basically set everything aside they could to help secure a future for their children (through a college education) and for themselves.

Their children grew oh-so-fast, and before they knew it, high school came and went. With tears in their eyes, they sent their children off to college, paid for by money saved so many years ago. They couldn't have been prouder as all three graduated from college without too many hiccups and started off on their own lives.

John and Sara were now empty-nesters. Retirement planning was front and center, with them now in their fifties. It was time to focus 100 percent on their financial goals, and they really began to put some serious money away, while also paying down every debt.

Their goals were simple: retire debt free (including the house) and never have to worry about money.

John and Sara had a clear vision of how they wanted to

live the second half of their lives. They wanted to travel, spend time with their children (and grandchildren), play golf and tennis, and volunteer at their church. For John and Sara, retirement was going to be fantastic!

Sara had always let John handle the investments. She took care of the kids and paid the household bills. John was the one who had the big 401(k) at work, anyway. She trusted him to do what was right for the two of them, and why shouldn't she?

John, for his part, *loved* investing. He was a big fan of the stock market. Over the years of his career at IBM, he put most of his money in stocks. Sure, there were years where he lost some money, but boy oh boy, the good years more than made up for the bad! John saw his 401(k) grow and grow, primarily driven through the growth of the stock market.

As John neared retirement, he had decades of successful investing behind him. As a result, when John and Sara finally retired, they did so full of confidence. The two of them had built up a nice nest egg totaling over $1 million in John's 401(k). When they did the math, they figured that they would only need to take $50,000 of income out each year—5 percent.

Given John's track record of growing their nest egg, retirement should've been easy. They saw no need to hire a Financial Advisor. Why should they? Clearly, John was good at this.

DID THEIR RETIREMENT WORK OUT?

John and Sara happily and confidently entered into retirement with excitement in their eyes. They started travelling immediately with a bucket list trip to Europe, followed by a relaxing Caribbean cruise. Then, off to see their new grandchild.

Life was great!

But a funny thing happened along the way.

You see, John and Sara happened to retire during a bit of an economic downturn. The year was 2000, when the stock market began to go through one of its down cycles.

When John and Sara returned home from seeing their new grandchild, John opened his investment statements and saw that his $1 million 401(k) was now down in the $900,000s. *No big deal*, he thought. *We've seen this story more than once over the years. Things will get better.* John put it out of his mind and didn't bother to mention anything to Sara, as he didn't want her to be upset for no reason.

John and Sara continued on in their retirement, following all the pursuits they had talked about. And the down cycle of the economy and the stock market continued as well.

John watched his account balances continue to fall, but he still wasn't too worried, as he had seen this happen before. Markets always get better. You just have to give them time.

And John just let it go—until he was three years into his retirement, and suddenly his $1 million IRA was now below $600,000. Sara wanted to go on another cruise, but John started thinking that perhaps they should tighten their belts a bit.

This is when John had the "opportunity" to have the very uncomfortable conversation with Sara about the state of their finances. Once Sara found out that their retirement accounts were down below $600,000—well, you can imagine.

John and Sara were only three years into their retirement. And over 40 percent of the money they had worked their entire lives to save was gone. They had envisioned an exciting retirement. Now, they went to bed each night wondering whether their money would actually last for another twenty to thirty years.

HOW DID THEIR STORY END?

Several years went by. Markets did improve, which helped John and Sara out, but then things went south again (you remember 2008). The second market downturn really depleted their savings. Shortly thereafter, John tragically had a stroke and passed away, leaving Sara alone.

Sara is still alive today, but her retirement doesn't resemble anything she ever expected. That $1 million portfolio is now below $100,000. She is doing her best to squeak by on Social Security and a small pension left over from John's job at IBM.

Things have gotten so bad, she is starting to look at selling the home and downsizing. She is afraid of becoming a burden on her children, something no parent would ever want.

John and Sara entered into retirement full of confidence. Just a few short years in, the world turned on them. Their retirement ended up much different than they ever imagined. Where did they go wrong?

HOW COULD THIS HAVE HAPPENED?

Here we have a couple who did everything the way they thought they were supposed to do while planning their retirement. They were good people, hard workers, and not big spenders (compared to their savings). They thought they had saved up a good amount of money, and they retired with the equivalent of over $1 million. Somehow, though, they ended up with nothing. John and Sara's story repeats throughout America over the years, as it unfortunately happens over and over again to good, hard-working families.

You see, when John and Sara retired, their lives changed. Moving from working (receiving a regular paycheck) and into retirement (twenty to thirty years of unemployment) represented *a fundamental shift in life*.

It's a time when you are both no longer being paid for working and you are no longer adding money to your retirement savings. It's quite the opposite. Instead of adding money to your savings, you are now taking money out for income.

When you reach this fundamental shift in life, you need to change your investment strategy because you now have different goals. Yet, millions of Americans don't make that shift, just as John and Sara didn't. Because of that, there's a real chance they'll run out of money, too.

The majority of people in or near retirement are in the same situation. Think back to the markets of 2008. Didn't *everyone* lose close to half of their portfolio?

Imagine being retired during a period like that. Not only are you losing money to market conditions, but you are also taking money out for income. You would be selling positions to create cash for your retirement needs, right at the worst time—when markets are low.

This is exactly how to crush your retirement, and the opposite of what you should be doing.

This book is written to help you gain a new perspective on how to invest during your retirement years. A fundamental shift in life requires a fundamental shift in your retirement savings. The good news is that I will be sharing time-tested strategies so you can live an exciting retirement, regardless of what markets throw your way.

How is it that people today are still doing the same thing John and Sara did, and why haven't we learned from the retirement planning mistakes they made? I see intelligent people making the same mistakes over and over again. The purpose of this book is to help you avoid making these same mistakes, so that when the next financial catastrophe hits the markets—*and history tells us that it eventually will*—you will be better prepared to ride out the volatility and continue enjoying the retirement lifestyle you worked all your life to achieve.

I began my career helping families with their retirement

planning on June 27, 1995. Over the last twenty-plus years, I've seen a lot. Markets have gone up and markets have gone down. I've learned many things, but one above all others: successful investing during your retirement years is a completely different ballgame than what you have experienced before.

Why did John and Sara's retirement plan fail them? The answer to that question is the core foundation of this book. In the next chapter, I'll present the details of why their planning went sideways in their later years. We'll look at why their retirement funds didn't last as long as needed, and we'll begin to break down the many myths and inaccuracies of retirement planning that have become standardized information within the financial industry.

CHAPTER 2

John and Sara: What Went Wrong?

Before I dive into the specifics of what went wrong with John and Sara's retirement plan, let's first look at the economics of 2000, the year they retired.

From 1980 to the end of 1999, Americans saw something they had never seen before—a twenty-year bull run. The stock market averaged approximately 14 percent per year positive gains over that twenty-year cycle. Amazing!

This huge run up, however, "taught" us a number of lessons that were not true.

1. Markets always go up over time (true). The problem is the definition of "time." We need to be thinking along the lines of fifteen or twenty years, whereas

by the end of the 1990s, we were "taught" that five years was plenty.

2. One only needs to hold stocks to be a successful investor. Why waste money on bonds and other guaranteed accounts that don't pay you anything?

3. The Vanguard® S&P 500 fund is all you ever need to own to be a successful investor.

As a result of the run up in the 1980s and 1990s, and the false lessons "learned," millions of Americans retiring in 2000 ended up just like John and Sara. They trusted the stock market too much.

Then, 2000 brought us the beginning of the dot-com crash. The NASDAQ, along with many tech companies, lost 80 percent of its value over the next three years. The stock market, as a whole, lost 43 percent.

On top of that, imagine taking distributions of 5 percent per year. Over three years, that is 15 percent of your money distributed out. It's no wonder so many Americans found their retirement accounts cut in half over that three-year period. Or worse.

After averaging roughly 14 percent per year for twenty years, the next ten years (2000–2009) brought us a stock market that earned absolutely nothing. Yet, John and Sara were still pulling money out.

I know, I know. *That was then*, you say, *and this is now. It's a different world now.*

Or is it?

What does the stock market of the early 2000s have to do with you and your retirement planning?

The story of how John and Sara ended up with nothing is meant to illustrate the critical need for a fundamental shift in the strategies used to manage your portfolio. That shift is accomplished by changing the way your portfolio is structured when you reach retirement.

THE FINANCIAL PLANNING PROCESS

To understand how this shift works, I like to use something I call the Financial Planning Process. It is easy to understand, and uses that crazy thing we all like to call common sense.

Goals	Strategies	Tools
Travel	Growth Strategy	Stocks/Mutual Funds
Spend Time with Family	Asset Allocation Strategy	Annuities
Stable Income	Income Strategy	Limited Partnerships
Protect Nest Egg	Principle Protection Strategy	Real Estate

INVESTMENT TOOLS

Here's how it works. Let's start with looking at the chart with three vertical columns. On the right-hand side of the chart is a column labeled "Tools." There are a lot of places you can invest your money, and they all fall in this column.

Here is a partial list of different tools you can use when building your portfolio:

- Stocks
- Bonds
- Mutual Funds

- Exchange Traded Funds (ETFs)
- Closed End Funds
- Limited Partnerships
- Annuities (Fixed, Variable, and Indexed)
- Options
- Commodities
- Futures
- Life Insurance
- Real Estate
- CDs
- Money Markets

As you can imagine, you have a ton of tools to choose from. Each has its own risk/return characteristics.

In John's case, he went with stocks and mutual funds that held stocks. That was about it.

One of the biggest problems we have in the financial world is that most Financial Advisors focus on this column. They want to sell you the latest and greatest hot stock, or hot annuity, or hot fill-in-the-blank.

This also holds true for all the financial media. Just watch CNBC for a while, and you'll see that their entire focus is on what tool is hot and what tool is not.

INVESTMENT STRATEGIES

The chart's middle column is labeled "Strategies." There are a number of strategies you may employ in your planning.

Examples include:

- Growth Strategy
- Asset Allocation Strategy
- Principal Protection Strategy
- Income Strategy
- Inflation Strategy
- Tax Strategy
- Debt Reduction Strategy
- Estate Distribution Strategy
- Charitable Planning Strategy

Just like the "Tools" column, each strategy has its own purpose.

INVESTMENT GOALS

Now let's look at that left-side column labeled "Goals."

This is, quite frankly, where you *should* spend most of your time. Unfortunately, it's also where the financial industry spends the least amount of time.

For John and Sara, when they were working, their goal

was to retire someday. But once they retired, their goal was to enjoy their retirement and not worry about money.

These two goals are very different!

HOW THE FINANCIAL PLANNING PROCESS WORKS

You start with your Goals. That should be obvious, but for some reason the financial world forgets this all too often. So, I will say it again—**start with your goals.**

Once you are clear on your goals, the next step is to identify which strategies you need to put into place to support your goals.

Then, when you have your strategies in place, the tools become obvious.

Let's see how this would have applied to John and Sara.

BACK TO JOHN AND SARA

When John and Sara were working, their goals were focused on paying for college and funding their retirement. These goals require strategies focusing on growth and accumulation.

When you are utilizing growth strategies, using tools like

stocks and/or stock mutual funds makes sense. This is what John did, so we can give him an A+ grade for planning correctly during that period of his life.

But then John and Sara went off the rails.

When they retired, their goals changed drastically. They wanted to live an exciting retirement. They wanted to travel, see their children and grandchildren, play golf and tennis, and volunteer at their church.

But while their goals changed, John did not change either his financial strategies or his financial tools. The result—failure.

What should John have done differently?

Well, now that we see the goals that he and Sara have for their retirement, we can quickly recognize that they need more than just a growth strategy. For example, they will need income from their retirement savings, so that leads to adding in an income strategy.

They also, whether they realize it or not, need a principal protection strategy. How about an inflation strategy, and a tax strategy? What about a healthcare strategy?

Are you starting to see how your financial planning during

retirement is a lot harder than when you are simply working and trying to grow your savings?

If we can agree that John and Sara should have been re-thinking their goals and strategies, what does that mean for the tools that John should have been using in his portfolio? That's right—he needed to diversify far outside of what he was familiar with during the growth phase of his planning.

Now...what about you?

If you are within five years of retirement, it's time to start shifting.

I see people in my office every day who are closing in on retirement and have their portfolio in a 401(k) or other similar investment tool. That worked perfectly through their working years as a growth tool, but if they fail to make that fundamental shift, they will end up just like John and Sara.

When I run their portfolios through an analysis program, such as Morningstar, I usually find that 70 percent or more of their money is in the stock market. In other words, they are investing like John did, and that will eventually get them in trouble.

Are you like them?

I would understand their investment structure if they were doing this all on their own. But many of them have a Financial Advisor who put them in this position! This is a common problem in our industry. Most Financial Advisors are trained in building a portfolio for you that focuses on a growth strategy. This is fine while you are working.

But if you are within five years of retirement, it's not fine anymore. It never hurts to have someone with a higher understanding of retirement planning give you a second opinion.

WHAT DOES YOUR PORTFOLIO LOOK LIKE?

Let me introduce you to "Steve" and "Diane," a couple who came into my office recently. They had just retired; he was sixty-six, she was sixty-three. They had a Financial Advisor they'd been working with for the past twenty years, but came to my firm because they wanted a second opinion on their retirement plan. They wanted to be sure what they were doing was the best strategy going forward.

What I found is typical of so many people I see in my office. When they met with their Financial Advisor, they would sit down, look at their portfolio, and see how it was doing against the market. Steve and Diane felt something was missing, and they were right. When I asked if their Financial Advisor ever talked to them about tax planning or income planning, like so many others, the answer was, "No, all we talked about was the portfolio's performance."

This is where I shared the Financial Planning Process and the three-column chart. We talked about their goals, which then led to a discussion on strategies and tools. Their advisor was focused only on the right-hand column, the tools. I had a frank discussion with them about the left-hand column—their goals—which was a perfect segue into discussing the extremely important middle column: their strategies.

Steve and Diane found this process to be clear and simple. And best of all, it made sense to them. Fortunately, our discussion was the launch pad that allowed them to fundamentally shift at a critical time for their retirement.

Here's another case. A very nice woman (we'll call her "Jane") came into my office in early 2000 with a great example of how large brokerage houses can steer an investor in the wrong direction. She was nearing retirement with a portfolio of $1.5 million, and her advisor had her invested in forty companies. She thought she was diversified, but they were all tech stocks. I tried to tell her that having all stocks invested in one sector was a bad idea. But this was a time where everything her advisor put her in made money. She thanked me for my time, but made no changes.

A bit more than two years later, at the end of 2002, after the tech markets suffered huge losses, Jane came to me and said, "Okay, I didn't listen to you and now I have to eat crow. I'm ready to move over to you." I found out that her $1.5 million had gone all the way down to $300,000. Over 80 percent of her money was gone within two years, and she was buying all the way down.

In the two weeks it took her to move the money over to my firm, another $50,000 evaporated. From $1.5 million, she was now down to $250,000 because she did the exactly the same things millions of Americans still do today. These Financial Advisors out there talk about diversification, but they don't practice it.

Jane did not fundamentally shift early enough, she didn't consider all three columns in the Financial Planning Process, and a large portion of her retirement money was gone forever.

Now that we understand what happened to John and Sara—*and so many other investors at or near retirement age*—we're ready to talk about the secrets to investing successfully during retirement. It comes down to knowing when to make that fundamental shift, and learning which tools to use in order to implement the right strategies and make sure your retirement goals become reality.

CHAPTER 3

How to Get It Right?

The first step to make the necessary shift in your retirement planning is to fully understand the Financial Planning Process we discussed in chapter two, which lays out your retirement goals, the strategies needed to attain those goals, and the tools required to make the strategies perform well.

Now it's time to shift to a discussion of investing, and how to get it right for your retirement.

When my dad retired, he came to me with his 401(k) and gave me three simple rules:

1. Protect your principal.
2. Get some income.
3. If you can, grow it a bit.

How does that sound to you for your money during your retirement? Most people tell me that it works for them! Some though, tell me that it's ok to spend their children's inheritance. And that's fine too.

With that in mind, let's see how different portfolios do with those directives during good times and bad.

EIGHTY-EIGHT MILES AN HOUR

In one of the most successful movie franchises of all time—1985's *Back to the Future*—Doc Brown devises a plan to travel through time. When the DeLorean is combined with a plutonium-powered flux capacitor and accelerates to eighty-eight miles per hour, 1.21 gigawatts of power is generated, allowing Doc and Marty to travel into the past or the future.

How does this movie relate to your retirement planning? You'll see...

Imagine that on December 31, 2016, I pull into your driveway in Doc's DeLorean, knock on your front door, and ask you to take a little trip with me back in time. We travel back to January 1, 2000, because that's the day my father (and John and Sara) retired. Strap yourself in, we are driving that baby to eighty-eight miles per hour, and I'll even let you drive. Ready? Here we go!

In a nanosecond, we arrive at January 1, 2000. We step out of the DeLorean and I give you $1 million. You'll have the opportunity to invest that money in one of two accounts. You have to pick either Account #1 or Account #2. Once you choose, you will put your entire $1 million into that account, and we'll only remain in the year 2000 for as long as it takes to deposit the money, about five minutes. This money will now begin to grow tax-free until we've cranked up the DeLorean again and return to your present-day driveway, where you can open your account and retrieve your money. Simple enough?

Here are the rules...

When I give you the $1 million, you have to invest ALL the money in Account #1 or Account #2. The cool part is that we are from the future, so we know in advance that if you put this money into Account #1, over the next sixteen to seventeen years, it will average a 6 percent annual rate of return. If you choose to put that money into Account #2, it will also earn 6 percent a year. Since both accounts pay you the same 6 percent return, how do you choose? And does it even matter?

The answer is YES, it does matter.

Let me give you another piece of information. Pretend we know the names of these companies managing the money because we're from the future. If you put your money in Account #1, a company called Vanguard® will manage that money. They have a terrific reputation, we know they keep costs low, and everybody says they're a great firm.

If you choose Account #2, a hypothetical company called XYZ Management will handle your money. You have never heard of this company, but you know you can earn 6 percent a year with both Vanguard® or with XYZ. However, it is not certain whether XYZ will exist in the future. Does this influence your choice?

Everyone I've ever asked says they would select Vanguard®. I agree with them 100 percent. Both firms will get you the same return, and one you know and one you don't. Simple decision.

So now that you've invested your $1 million in Vanguard®, we hop back into the DeLorean, pump the accelerator up to eighty-eight miles per hour, and go back to the future, arriving on December 31, 2016, where we started. You open your investment statement to see how your $1 million has grown.

Your statement tells you that your $1 million investment placed in the account managed by Vanguard® has grown to $2,078,000. Your money has doubled! How does this make you feel? Most people say they feel pretty good.

But let's pretend on the day I took you back to January 1, 2000, that you chose Account #2 managed by XYZ Management who offered the same 6 percent return. Why did you do that? Maybe you were mad at Vanguard® for some reason that day. Maybe you were feeling in the mood to fight the establishment. Who knows?

Nevertheless, you chose account #2. We travel back to the future and open the XYZ statement on December 31, 2016 and discover you have accumulated over $2.6 million! You've earned over $500,000 more from XYZ even though both accounts offered the exact same 6 percent average rate of return. This is fantastic, but how did it happen?

To understand how this happened, we have to do a little math. It all has to do with an important term: *variance*.

VARIANCE

Variance may be the most important topic discussed in this entire book. It is well worth your time to learn about variance because *this is the secret deciding factor between succeeding in retirement and failing.* To understand what variance is, let's consider an individual stock that is up 60 percent the first year, but down 40 percent the next. The difference between +60 percent and -40 percent is the *variance* of 100 percent. For those two years, the average return would have been 10 percent per year (+60% - 40% = 20%/2 years = 10%/year).

Now, consider a diversified portfolio that is up 30 percent the first year and down 10 percent the second year—it yields the same 10 percent average return (+30% - 10% = 20%/2 years = 10%/year). However, the variance of +30 percent to -10 percent is only 40 percent versus the example for an individual stock that had a variance of 100 percent.

Let's see how you would do with each:

Investment	Return Rate	End Balance
$100,000	+60%	$160,000
$160,000	-40%	$96,000
$100,000	+30%	$130,000
$130,000	-10%	$117,000

Same average rate of return...different results!

THE GOLDEN SECRET

When you compare two portfolios with the same average rate of return, *the one with the lower variance always gives you more money.* When we went back to the future, if you had picked Account #1 and started with $1 million, you would have ended with $2 million. That portfolio—the

Vanguard® S&P 500 index (and the same type of account John put his money in)—had a variance year in, year out of 69 percent. The best year was +32 percent, and the worst year was -37 percent. The difference between them is a variance of 69 percent.

You can see the year-by-year results and how this account grew over time in Table 3.1.

Table 3.1

Year	Portfolio 1	Beg Bal	Earnings	Withdrawal	End Bal
2000	-9.06%	$1,000,000	-$90,600	$0	$909,400
2001	-12.02%	$909,400	-$109,310	$0	$800,090
2002	-22.15%	$800,090	-$177,220	$0	$622,870
2003	28.50%	$622,870	$177,518	$0	$800,388
2004	10.74%	$800,388	$85,962	$0	$886,350
2005	4.77%	$886,350	$42,279	$0	$928,629
2006	15.64%	$928,629	$145,238	$0	$1,073,866
2007	5.39%	$1,073,866	$57,881	$0	$1,131,748
2008	-37.02%	$1,131,748	-$418,973	$0	$712,775
2009	26.49%	$712,775	$188,814	$0	$901,589
2010	14.91%	$901,589	$134,427	$0	$1,036,016
2011	1.97%	$1,036,016	$20,410	$0	$1,056,425
2012	15.82%	$1,056,425	$167,126	$0	$1,223,552
2013	32.18%	$1,223,552	$393,739	$0	$1,617,290
2014	13.51%	$1,617,290	$218,496	$0	$1,835,786
2015	1.25%	$1,835,786	$22,947	$0	$1,858,734
2016	11.82%	$1,858,734	$219,702	$0	$2,078,436
Average	6.04%				

Account #2 from XYZ Management is an example of the typical portfolio that we build for our clients. The best year for Account #2 was only up 19 percent; however, the worst year was only down 2 percent. The difference between those two years illustrates a portfolio with a variance of 21 percent.

Account #2 is detailed in Table 3.2.

Table 3.2

Year	Portfolio 2	Beg Bal	Earnings	Withdrawal	End Bal
2000	3.78%	$1,000,000	$37,800	$0	$1,037,800
2001	-0.98%	$1,037,800	-$10,204	$0	$1,027,595
2002	0.27%	$1,027,595	$2,728	$0	$1,030,323
2003	19.20%	$1,030,323	$197,820	$0	$1,228,143
2004	9.67%	$1,228,143	$118,730	$0	$1,346,873
2005	6.51%	$1,346,873	$87,732	$0	$1,434,606
2006	11.17%	$1,434,606	$160,256	$0	$1,594,862
2007	5.28%	$1,594,862	$84,130	$0	$1,678,992
2008	-1.74%	$1,678,992	-$29,251	$0	$1,649,741
2009	10.96%	$1,649,741	$180,768	$0	$1,830,509
2010	8.22%	$1,830,509	$150,530	$0	$1,981,039
2011	5.10%	$1,981,039	$101,097	$0	$2,082,136
2012	8.13%	$2,082,136	$169,219	$0	$2,251,355
2013	8.16%	$2,251,355	$183,774	$0	$2,435,129
2014	7.74%	$2,435,129	$188,484	$0	$2,623,613
2015	-2.17%	$2,623,613	-$57,040	$0	$2,566,572
2016	3.33%	$2,566,572	$85,343	$0	$2,651,915
Average	6.04%				

Both accounts #1 and #2 had the same average return of 6 percent, but the variance of the two accounts were very different (#1 at 69 percent versus #2 at 21 percent). And remember, *the lower variance always wins*. Because of its lower variance, Account #2 yielded a difference of an additional $500,000.

That's a big win.

Do you have a Financial Advisor? If so, you need to ask that person what the variance is on your portfolio. You might also want to ask them why it's *your* job to bring this question to their attention.

Here is another thought. Shouldn't your advisor tell you what the variance is of the portfolio they are recommending before you give them your money? This is a key point to understand because in our *Back to the Future* example, we were simply putting money into two different portfolios and letting it ride. However, had you picked the portfolio with the lower variance, you would have earned an additional $500,000.

To really understand variance and how it can contribute to your desire to retire well, I'd like to dive deeper into what many initial visits to your typical Financial Advisor are often like, and discuss what is really going on when you sit down and they begin to review your paperwork.

Typically, compliance departments within any big investment firm require that a new client fill out a risk profile questionnaire. Questions can include:

- How old are you?
- How long do you want your money to last?
- When are you going to start taking income?
- How much risk are you willing to take?

Just so you are aware, these risk profile questionnaires offer no benefit to you, the client. Rather, they are 100 percent designed to protect the firm from any liability in the event you suffer financial loss. Advisors are required to administer these questionnaires by the firm's attorneys.

The most problematic issue is that their advisors use this questionnaire to create a plan, calling it an *asset allocation strategy*. They ask their clients to choose from a colorful pie chart to fill out their portfolio. Typically, these pie pieces are mutual funds or something similar. This is standard procedure to sell certain investment tools where the company makes the most profit. You will notice the term variance never comes up in this discussion.

This is completely backwards to the way I serve a client. The big firms in the financial industry start with the tools portion of the Financial Planning Process and work their way around to serving a client's goals. Advisors like myself start with a client's goals and find the right tools to achieve those goals, using the strategies that are the best fit.

This chapter's purpose was to give you a good idea of the importance of a portfolio's variance—it is the most critical element to consider when accomplishing your desire to retire well. If your Financial Advisor is not openly discussing variance from the first visit, maybe it's time to start shopping for someone else, someone who fully understands every aspect of a proper retirement financial plan.

CHAPTER 4

How Does Variance Coordinate with Your Income Planning?

If you *don't* need income from your retirement portfolio today, that is fantastic, but like every investor, you probably still want to protect your principle and grow the account. You may not need income right now, but growing the account represents future security. It can protect you against healthcare expenses down the road or allow you to leave an inheritance for your children or grandchildren. Sadly, most people retiring today rely solely on Social Security and their retirement savings, which, as we have discovered, are not enough to retire well with the financial stability you had hoped to enjoy.

In the last chapter, we discussed the impact that variance

has on a portfolio. We examined two portfolios, each starting with $1 million on the day my father retired (January 1, 2000), and after letting those hypothetical accounts grow until the end of 2016, we compared the results.

In this chapter, we will delve deeper into the subject of variance, something that must be understood to retire well.

REAL WORLD CASE STUDY

My father worked as a claims adjuster with State Farm Insurance for over thirty years, and, after putting four children through college, retired on January 1, 2000, with a pension, Social Security, and a 401(k) plan. His retirement planning is probably not unlike many people reading this book. I know this because I see these people come into my office every day.

In reality, my father did not have $1 million when he retired, but let's pretend he did for the sake of this discussion. Imagine that he wanted to withdraw $50,000 a year for income in retirement. You might say that $50,000 a year on a million-dollar portfolio seems like too much. In today's world, that is a lot to pull from a million-dollar portfolio because interest rates are so low, but in 2000, there were ten-year CDs paying 7 percent per year. The stock market from 1980 to 2000 averaged 14 percent a year. In that type of environment, withdrawing $50,000 a year from a $1 million portfolio is perfectly acceptable.

Let's break this down and see some of the differences.

THE ACCOUNT #1 APPROACH

Looking back at the *Back to the Future* scenario from Chapter 3, let's again examine portfolio one, the Vanguard® approach. All the big money magazines of the day recommended investing in the stock market, specifically in the Vanguard® S&P 500. The stock market always goes up and when it goes down, it's only for a short period of time, they said. Millions of Americans were putting their money in the Vanguard® S&P 500—they had so much blind faith in the market in those days.

Let's say those investors started pulling out $50,000 a year for retirement income, and adjusted each year for inflation. Each year, they increased their income by 2 percent and withdrew $50,000 the first year, $51,000 the next year, and so on.

If I had put my father's hypothetical $1 million in that Vanguard® S&P 500 portfolio in 2000, and he pulled out $50,000 or more inflation-adjusted funds to live on each year, he would have had just $92,000 left in his retirement account by the end of 2016 when he was eighty years old. That amount would give him, at most, a year and a half of income.

See Table 4.1 for a detailed breakdown.

Table 4.1

Year	Portfolio 1	Beg Bal	Earnings	Withdrawal	End Bal
2000	-9.06%	$1,000,000	-$90,600	-$50,000	$859,400
2001	-12.02%	$859,400	-$103,300	-$51,000	$705,100
2002	-22.15%	$705,100	-$156,180	-$52,020	$496,900
2003	28.50%	$496,900	$141,617	-$53,060	$585,457
2004	10.74%	$585,457	$62,878	-$54,122	$594,213
2005	4.77%	$594,213	$28,344	-$55,204	$567,353
2006	15.64%	$567,353	$88,734	-$56,308	$599,779
2007	5.39%	$599,779	$32,328	-$57,434	$574,673
2008	-37.02%	$574,673	-$212,744	-$58,583	$303,346
2009	26.49%	$303,346	$80,356	-$59,755	$323,948
2010	14.91%	$323,948	$48,301	-$60,950	$311,298
2011	1.97%	$311,298	$6,133	-$62,169	$255,262
2012	15.82%	$255,262	$40,383	-$63,412	$232,233
2013	32.18%	$232,233	$74,733	-$64,680	$242,285
2014	13.51%	$242,285	$32,733	-$65,974	$209,044
2015	1.25%	$209,044	$2,613	-$67,293	$144,363
2016	11.82%	$144,363	$17,064	-$68,639	$92,788
Average	6.04%				

Imagine that he went to the doctor and the doctor said, "Congratulations, you're in great shape. You're going to live another ten years." Instead of feeling joyful upon hearing this news, my father would be depressed, thinking, "Great, I'm going to live ten more years, but my money is only going to last a year and a half."

Millions of retirees who made the same investment decisions as he did are in this position today. Putting all of your money in the markets during retirement does not work. One would think that we would have learned from our mistakes by now.

Remember, this is the approach that John and Sara took at the beginning of the book.

As humans, experience has always been our greatest teacher. Ironically, it seems we don't learn from our mistakes when it comes to money. Every day, I see a parade of sixty-five to seventy-year-olds walk in to our office with big portfolios representing all the major brokerage houses. They have 70 percent to 80 percent of their money invested in the stock market. They have the rest invested in what they think are bonds because they believe it's safer. However, they are actually invested in high-yield bonds, also known as *junk bonds*. They might as well have put it in the market for the risk they are taking. Essentially, these people still have 100 percent of their money in the market.

XYZ MANAGEMENT

Now consider the same scenario with our imaginary company, XYZ Management (how we manage money at my firm). Say my father retired with the same hypothetical $1 million, started taking $50,000 a year as income, and increased that 2 percent per year for inflation. Now remember that XYZ's portfolio had a lower variance. As a result of the lower variance, if my father had chosen that approach in 2000, he'd have a little over $1 million left at the end of 2016! He would have protected his principal, taken income, and grown his account, achieving all three of his goals.

See Table 4.2 for a detailed breakdown.

Table 4.2

Year	Portfolio 2	Beg Bal	Earnings	Withdrawal	End Bal
2000	3.78%	$1,000,000	$37,800	-$50,000	$987,800
2001	-0.98%	$987,800	-$9,713	-$51,000	$927,087
2002	0.27%	$927,087	$2,461	-$52,020	$877,528
2003	19.20%	$877,528	$168,484	-$53,060	$992,951
2004	9.67%	$992,951	$95,993	-$54,122	$1,034,823
2005	6.51%	$1,034,823	$67,406	-$55,204	$1,047,025
2006	11.17%	$1,047,025	$116,960	-$56,308	$1,107,677
2007	5.28%	$1,107,677	$58,431	-$57,434	$1,108,673
2008	-1.74%	$1,108,673	-$19,315	-$58,583	$1,030,775
2009	10.96%	$1,030,775	$112,946	-$59,755	$1,083,967
2010	8.22%	$1,083,967	$89,139	-$60,950	$1,112,156
2011	5.10%	$1,112,156	$56,756	-$62,169	$1,106,743
2012	8.13%	$1,106,743	$89,947	-$63,412	$1,133,278
2013	8.16%	$1,133,278	$92,507	-$64,680	$1,161,105
2014	7.74%	$1,161,105	$89,872	-$65,974	$1,185,003
2015	-2.17%	$1,185,003	-$25,763	-$67,293	$1,091,946
2016	3.33%	$1,091,946	$36,309	-$68,639	$1,059,616
Average	6.04%				

So why doesn't everyone put their money into portfolio two, the one with much lower variance offered by advisors like my firm? Because it's not exciting. Quite frankly, financial media outlets are not interested in reporting on such technical topics as variance; they instead focus on splashy articles about big name stocks and funds. This is important to consider as the media holds immense sway on how people invest their money.

The many print and electronic financial media outlets need something to talk about, but only if it's exciting, creates interest, and drives readership and viewership.

In reality, you want to be boring when it comes to your money.

You want to choose a low volatility, diversified approach with a much lower variance. Your goal for your portfolio as you near and enter into retirement is to be boring, because a boring portfolio helps you focus on enjoying an exciting life.

TOOLS OF THE TRADE

How do you build an effectively diversified portfolio? Most people get a job and start saving money for retirement. They make automatic contributions from their paycheck into their company retirement plan, whether it's a 401(k), a 403(b), a 457, an IRA, etc. For this example, we'll use the 401(k). Recognize that all those other plans are similar.

When you open a 401(k), the management company gives you a menu of options, including a list of available mutual funds. At this early stage, you're thinking about growing your money. Your overall goal is to make this portfolio as big as possible so that someday you can retire comfortably. For ten, twenty, maybe even forty years, you keep adding money and watch your portfolio grow until you get close to retirement. As you look at the numbers, you think if this continues, you should be able to retire within the next couple of years.

However, a little voice inside your head reminds you about those few times in the last twenty years when the market crashed. You begin thinking about 2008, the total debacle where the stock market lost half its value in less than two years. You convince yourself that since you're close to retirement, you'll be fine. But wait...what if the market collapses again and sheds half its value? You might end up working for the next seven or eight years to make up for all those losses, and that would be horrible.

Perhaps you've recently retired and are thinking the exact same thing...what if? Some recent retirees are advised to start moving their money into safer investments like Certificates of Deposits or low-yield bonds where they tie up their money for five or ten years and may only receive a 1 percent to 2 percent return. I often see some retirees leave a small amount in the markets where it's growth-oriented and maybe leave some money in cash. These investors are trying to find some safe middle ground, a happy medium between growth and safety.

The problem with this type of plan is it's often not executed efficiently, and it's not an effective form of diversification. Financial Advisors like myself with a specialty in retirement planning live in this middle ground area; the difference, though, is that we've learned the key steps to building a portfolio that is effectively diversified, one with low variance that achieves the goals needed to retire well.

HOW TO EFFECTIVELY DIVERSIFY
STEP ONE: PRINCIPAL/INCOME PROTECTION

The first step in proper diversification is to identify how much of your principal you want to protect in case the markets collapse. We can look at this in two ways. That amount might be 20 percent, 50 percent, or in some cases, as much as 80 percent. Regardless of the amount, you still need to get a decent return on this money. You simply can't put this money in an account where it would earn 1 percent, or even less, such as a CD or bank savings account.

If you open your mind to the variety of options available,

it is legitimately possible to get as much as a 3 percent to 6 percent annualized return on principal protection accounts. However, you have to be willing to give something up, because there's no such thing as a free lunch. If you want to get a higher rate of return on accounts where your money is guaranteed, you have to give up some liquidity.

In other words, if you put $100,000 in a guaranteed account where you're earning 3 percent to 6 percent rate of return, you have to be willing to leave that money there for up to ten years. During that time, you have to be willing to limit withdraws to a maximum of 5 percent to 10 percent per year or you'll be penalized for early withdrawals.

Accounts like this exist at various insurance companies. They normally fall under the general category of something called *fixed-indexed annuities.*

A recent study by famed investment researcher, Roger Ibbotson, PhD, actually put forth the argument that a retiree should eliminate all bonds in their portfolio and replace them with properly structured fixed-indexed annuities.[1] The conclusion of the study was that in today's world, a fixed-indexed annuity does the job of a bond better than bonds do.

---

1   Roger Ibbotson, PhD, "Fixed-Indexed Annuities: Consider the Alternative," January 2018.

With that being said, *it is crucial that you don't put a dime into any of these types of tools without first understanding all of the advantages and disadvantages*, because there are thousands of these particular tools and *all are not equal.*

Our firm continually conducts due diligence on annuities of this type, and has found only three or four of them that are worth using. Many top advisors throughout country commonly refer to these types of investment tools as part of *Alternative Asset Classes*, and I will get into more detail on them shortly.

STEP TWO: ALLOCATION

Now that you have a decent-sized portion of your portfolio protected, you can take some risk with the remainder to get a better return. The key lies in *allocations*, which fall into two categories: the first includes alternative assets; the second allocates across different management styles.

Alternative Assets

The different asset classes offered in a 401(k) are basically stocks, bonds, and cash. Occasionally you might see real estate, some commodities, or gold. To effectively diversify in this step, you need to expand far beyond the use of stocks, bonds, and cash. For example, you may want to think on a global scale with stocks and have both US and international positions present, as well as large and small companies. With bonds, you want both corporate and government. This is standard allocation, but it doesn't stop here.

Unlike the big brokerage houses, to properly diversify a retirement portfolio, your Financial Advisor needs to push further afield and include more alternatives. For example, real estate and gold should be included in every portfolio—you don't have to invest a lot in these categories, but you want them included. You also might want to consider what's called *Covered Call Writing*. People who have high net worth and own large stock portfolios often use this tool. They sell a *call option* to a third-party buyer, and if that stock goes up a certain amount, the third-party buys away that stock at a gain. However, if the stock doesn't go up, the seller keeps the stock. In that case, the third-party had to pay a premium for that option, so the seller has earned additional income on their stock portfolio.

There are also ways to diversify that might not come up in the conversations you've had with your current Financial Advisor. If you have sizable investments over $1 million, you may add alternatives like owning *billboards* or *cell towers* and leasing them out. You may be able to provide financing for apartment complexes at higher than normal bank rates, or provide factoring for attorneys. In this case, an attorney wins a lawsuit but won't get paid for six months, so you can fund that attorney 90 percent of their winnings and take the 100 percent when they get paid for a nice return.

There are countless alternatives to add to your portfolio. The key is to not put big bets in any one of them. It is better to spread your money across a lot of alternatives with smaller amounts in each. Listen to your Grandmother and don't put all your eggs in one basket.

Management Styles

There are stark differences in management styles when it comes to diversification. Let's say you want to add bonds into your portfolio and use a *bond manager* who purchases your assets in a bond fund solely based upon where they believe you'll make the most money for that category. That is one example of a more static management style.

Another type of bond manager will buy bonds from companies whose financial strength may have declined, but the big rating companies like Moody's and Standard & Poor's have listed those failing companies on a positive rate watch. In other words, they believe these companies are shaping up and their ratings are going to rise. Six months later, those companies are re-rated and their financial strength is increased. The minute this happens, the bonds those managers bought six months prior increase in value and the managers sell the bonds for a gain.

Both managers were holding "bonds," but they handle investments differently. It's impossible to tell which manager's strategy is going to perform better year-to-year, but if you hold them both, you will get better returns with less volatility, which leads to overall lower portfolio variance.

If you use this technique across all the various asset classes, you will effectively build a diversified portfolio. Combining various asset classes and using different management styles will reduce your risk portion and can produce nice returns. You should leave this area to the professionals who truly live their lives embedded in this environment. If alternative asset classes are used incorrectly, you can inadvertently increase your risk.

And when it comes to risk, it seems everyone knows somebody who invested in oil and gas and lost everything. This is called *exploratory investing*. It's sexy, sure, but also extremely dangerous. If executed properly, it can become a valuable strategy. One could instead invest in oil and gas, but on the development side with less risk. They've already found the oil and are currently developing the field. You won't make 30 percent to 40 percent as promised in the "sexy" scenario, but the risk of losing money is significantly less. Bingo—less overall variance.

STEP THREE: PLACEMENT

Placement simply refers to putting the right asset in the right tax account. I'll dive deeper into the complex subject of taxation later in the book, but for now, let's just examine the basics of how different ways of placing (allocating) your assets can make significant differences in your long-term financial stability.

Imagine you have money saved in a standard individual investment account, one that is not an IRA or tax-sheltered account. You've already paid tax on this income and put $10,000 in stocks where it grows to $20,000 over a period of years. This is a $10,000 gain. Because you held the stock for more than a year, when you sell those stocks, you will owe a long-term capital gains tax on that gain, typically 15 percent, depending on your income tax bracket.

What would have happened, though, if you had held that same stock in your tax-deferred IRA? You invested the same $10,000 and it grew to $20,000. At seventy and a half years of age, you'll be subject to *Required Minimum Distributions*, a federal regulation requiring you to begin withdrawing a certain amount each year. That money is now taxed as ordinary income, both federal and state, and could be upwards of 25 percent or even 30 percent. If you want to own stock, you obviously want to hold it where you pay less tax; thus, stocks tend to be more efficient when held outside of retirement accounts.

Placement is a critical consideration for any diversified retirement plan. Are you putting the right money in the right places? Not only that, are you pulling income from the right tax accounts at the right time? We'll talk more about taxes later, because it is a critical element of retiring well.

Those are some of the many steps needed to build a diversified portfolio—staying focused on consistency, being boring, keeping variance low, and protecting assets. In order to effectively employ this diversification strategy, you need to have saved up around $500,000 because there needs to be enough money to invest reasonable amounts in each of these different asset classes.

If you don't have that much saved, all is not lost. Anyone who has at least $100,000 can start to deploy 20 percent to 30 percent of their portfolio using these diversification techniques. A few options may be to include real estate or gold in your portfolio, and there are even mutual funds available today that handle these types of investments.

What is key to understand is that diversification can take many forms, with about as many different strategies as there are Financial Advisors in the industry. Whether you have a $100,000 portfolio or one well north of that number, finding someone with the breadth of knowledge needed to sift through the many tools available and build a personalized plan just for you is the most important thing you will do if retiring well is in your life plan.

CHAPTER 5

Create Your Retirement Income

INCOME EQUALS LIFESTYLE

One of the biggest mistakes I see when people plan their retirement is not focusing enough time and energy on stabilizing their retirement income. At the end of the day, your income equals your lifestyle, and in retirement, your lifestyle is entirely based on monthly cash flows. For most retirees, this comes from Social Security, pensions, real estate income, and stock portfolios.

When I started in the financial industry in the 1990s, pensions were common. Combined with Social Security, it often seemed like people never needed to touch their 401(k) and IRA retirement accounts. The only time they pulled money out is when they reached age seventy and a half and were forced to withdraw money per the required minimum distribution regulation. Around the 2000s, however, pensions started to disappear. Why did this happen?

During the 1980s and 1990s, there was a groundswell change regarding how companies provided for their employees' retirement. Many pension plans were eliminated to reduce company liability, and many became extinct because employees began asking employers to contribute to their 401(k) accounts instead. Employees believed they could make more money invested in stocks inside a 401(k) than traditional pension plans. Because of this shift, most people retiring today are relying entirely on Social Security and their 401(k) and 403(b) retirement plans.

Let's compare then and now. In the 1990s, my clients had Social Security and pensions when they retired, both of which are guaranteed income for life. Today, Social Security is still guaranteed income for life, but 401(k) s are not. It is critical to change our mindset about this. People say to me all the time, "It's no big deal if the markets collapse. I'll just tighten my belt. I won't go on that extra trip. I won't buy that new car. I don't need to go out to dinner as often."

Seriously?

Nobody should believe that a sound retirement plan includes "tightening your belt" because markets didn't cooperate. To believe that myth is like saying it's perfectly okay to have fun when the stock market is good and sit around the house doing nothing when it tanks.

Ask yourself this question: do you truthfully want your retirement lifestyle to be totally dependent on how the stock market behaves, or do you want to enjoy your retirement lifestyle whether markets are good or bad? Obviously, the latter.

I believe your retirement should be enjoyable, regardless of the stock market. Why should travel or time spent with your grandchildren depend on the roller coaster price changes of the stock market? Wouldn't you rather buy gifts for your family regardless of the stock market's performance?

When it comes to your retirement income planning, there are three key areas you need to focus on: basic income needs, inflation, and the extras. Let's cover these in a bit more detail.

BASE INCOME NEEDS

The first area is to identify your base income needs, such things as housing, transportation, insurance and food.

For example, you have to pay your mortgage, you need dependable transportation, and you have to eat—these are non-negotiable. Second, you must take a hard look at certain lifestyle bills and decide what you cannot live without. Certain hobbies may be continued or even increased in retirement, and the costs of these activities must be considered in this discussion.

INFLATION

The second is to recognize that because of inflation, the cost of living is not going to be the same tomorrow as it is today. To understand how inflation can affect your retirement income, let's look at three general timeframes and see how your spending will change during these stages.

THE "GO-GO" YEARS

The "Go-Go" years are your early retirement years, roughly defined as sixty-five to seventy-five years old. You're still young and healthy, and are actively pursuing interests you never could find the time to do before due to work and family obligations. You are out there enjoying life, learning to fly fish, or just learning to fly. This is the time you will likely spend the most money, short of significant healthcare needs later on. To make the most of this time, be sure to have some inflationary adjustments in place in your retirement financial plan.

THE "SLOW-GO" YEARS

The "Slow-Go" years are next. You've been retired for a number of years and traveled all over the world. You might be older than seventy-five and thinking you've been there, done that. You are becoming more selective in your pursuits. Perhaps you'll take a vacation because your really good friends invited you or there's a winery you've always wanted to explore. You're still out there doing things, just not quite at the same pace. Your needs are changing, and your financial plan needs to change as well.

THE "NO-GO" YEARS

Finally, you enter the "No-Go" years. You're probably eighty or older and perfectly happy just hanging around the house. You might have health issues that keep you from wandering too far from your doctor, so you don't travel like you once did. Many of your friends have started to pass on at this point. You are no longer motivated to get out there and see the world, and your need to pursue your "passion" hobbies and pastimes are no longer a priority.

The older you get with each stage, the more your spending in real dollars decreases. As a result, people in retirement rarely increase their spending over time at the same rate as inflation. Our office serves well over five hundred families, and I have yet to see one family increase their spending at a rate even equal to inflation, much less more than inflation. Nevertheless, it is important to recognize that inflation is still a real factor, and you need to accommodate for it in your portfolio.

EXTRAS

The third area, extras, basically includes the costs of everything else—the fun things in life like that bucket list vacation. I had a retired couple as clients whose dream was to take an around-the-world cruise. They hadn't yet made that journey because they didn't know if they could afford it. No Financial Advisor had shown them how to structure their money and set up an income plan, with base income and inflation accounted for, in order to allocate the extra money to take that dream vacation. They crunched numbers and estimated that it would cost about $40,000. Once we created their "Retiring Well" plan, they discovered they had $250,000 in extra money. They went on that dream vacation, knowing they were able to afford it. They were very happy clients.

REVIEW

When building a portfolio to support your income plan, first determine how much income you need to protect. If you want to maintain a certain lifestyle, that's your *goal*. You'll need to plan for a certain amount of cash flow coming every single month—that part of your portfolio is not going to be exciting, and that's okay. Its purpose is to deliver income consistently, regardless of market performance.

Next, you need to set money aside for inflation. This inflationary portion of your portfolio can be placed in more growth-oriented investment tools because you most likely won't need those funds until later in life. The rest of the money allocated for extras should be invested in something reasonably conservative.

Later in the book, I'll go over some portfolio building models to learn which part of your portfolio needs to be mostly conservative while allocating parts of it to growth investment tools. When you're ready to buy that new car or take that once-in-a-lifetime trip, you want the money available when it's needed, and your quality of life diminishes rapidly when you find out funds are no longer adequate to serve your needs. You want your portfolio to grow, but it needs to be reasonably safe as well. This is a balancing act best left to professionals who thoroughly understand retirement financial planning.

When building your retirement plan, begin by first asking yourself what you want to accomplish to achieve your goals. How you get from here to there—to retiring well— means taking the first steps to seek out someone who understands the many financial nuances of your retirement years. And like I have previously stated—but it's worth repeating—once you know your goals, all that is left is developing the right strategy to achieve them by using the right tools.

CHAPTER 6

Understanding Tax Categories

In the previous chapter, we explored the basics behind building a retirement income plan. One important component we haven't discussed in detail is the taxation of your income, and it is vital to recognize that different forms of retirement income will be taxed differently. The goal is to give the IRS as little as legally required. Most people feel they have paid enough to the IRS over the years and would like to pay less in their retirement.

There are three general categories of income taxation. Let's examine each one.

FULLY TAXABLE INCOME

The first is the fully taxable category. These income

streams count as ordinary income on your tax return and are equivalent to employee wages. Fully taxable cash flows are subject to some of the highest tax brackets, and this is a real consideration when building the right retirement financial plan.

PENSIONS

If you receive a pension, it is included in this category and taxed as ordinary income or wages. It is important to recognize that this is a tax obligation you will have for the rest of your life, as long as those pension checks keep coming in.

IRA/TAX-SHELTERED PLANS

Distributions from any tax-sheltered plans are taxed as ordinary income. These include funds from an IRA, 401(k), 403(b), 457, profit sharing plan, simple IRA, SEP IRA, etc. Every dollar you withdraw from any of these accounts as a distribution is fully taxed. There is, however, one exception that we'll cover later in this chapter.

PART-TIME EARNINGS

If you choose to work part-time during your retirement, your wages are considered a fully taxable stream of income. This is an important area to consider since this income may change your tax bracket, resulting in a higher tax bill.

RENTAL INCOME

Many people in retirement have investments in rental properties, and any income from these investments is fully taxable. Investing in a *Real Estate Investment Trust* (REIT) is another way to indirectly own real estate; however, the net proceeds from these trusts are also considered fully taxable income.

BOND INTEREST

Any interest earned on savings accounts, bank accounts, bonds, bond mutual funds, or even certain income mutual funds that you hold outside of retirement plans will generate a Form 1099 and is fully taxable. It is important to consider all of these income streams when preparing a financial plan for retirement.

SHORT-TERM CAPITAL GAINS

Short-term capital gains are when you buy stock, real estate, or any type of asset and sell within a year. I had a client with a valuable knife collection. If he bought a knife and sold it for a profit within one year, that would be considered a short-term capital gain and taxed as ordinary income.

NON-QUALIFIED DIVIDENDS

Non-qualified dividends come from many sources, but typically from mutual funds. These also include stocks that are held for less than one year and are taxed as fully taxable ordinary income. If you receive a Form 1099 or Form W-2 at the end of January from the institution sending you money, these are fully taxable. Other non-qualified dividends include earnings acquired from a limited partnership, or income from any type of business in which you are involved. Royalties are also considered ordinary income.

PARTIALLY TAXABLE INCOME

Category two includes income that is either partially taxable or taxed at lower rates. These streams of income are more tax-sufficient and also slightly more favored by the tax code.

SOCIAL SECURITY INCOME

In retirement, Social Security is the king of this category. Income from Social Security may not be taxed at all, but in many cases, up to 85 percent of that income may be subject to tax. We'll dive more into Social Security in a later chapter. Recognize that, as of this writing, no one pays tax on 100 percent of income from Social Security, as a minimum of 15 percent of Social Security income is always tax-free.

QUALIFIED DIVIDENDS

These are dividends received on stocks you've held for more than a year. If you buy ABC stock and hold it for more than a year and it pays a dividend, that dividend is taxed at long-term capital gains rates. In our current tax code, that might be 0 percent or as high as 20 percent, but generally speaking, it is less than the fully taxable category. You may be taxed on the entire amount but at a lower rate.

LONG-TERM CAPITAL GAINS

Like qualified dividends, if you buy stock and hold it for more than a year before selling at a profit, you're taxed on the total profit but at a lower rate.

ANNUITIES

Annuities have some interesting tax rules. If they are held outside of an IRA, they are tax-sheltered like an IRA, so the gains are not taxed. You only pay tax on the money you withdraw. However, depending on how you pull money out of an annuity, it may be fully taxable or partially taxable. It all depends on the method of withdrawal. Typically, annuities fall into this second category; withdrawals are partially taxable and partially tax-free. Because of the complexities of taxation regarding annuities, I will dive deeper into this topic later in the book.

TAX-FREE INCOME

The third and final category is our favorite. Income from these items is completely tax-free, and as part of a retirement financial plan that is designed correctly, this is the most important category to consider.

MUNICIPAL BONDS

Everyone thinks municipal bonds are completely tax-free. It is true that the interest earned on these bonds is tax-free. However, the interest does count against the tax that you pay on Social Security.

I have an interesting story to illustrate this ambiguity. My clients, "Doug" and "Kim," were living solely on their pensions and Social Security, and literally owed zero income tax at the end of every year. Their pensions and Social Security were perfectly structured. Pensions are normally fully taxable and Social Security is up to 85 percent taxable, but they had designed them to be zero percent taxable. It was fantastic!

Sadly, Kim's mother passed away and left her a municipal bond portfolio worth $300,000 with a 5 percent yield. Essentially, Kim received $300,000 in municipal bonds, tax-free. They were also generating tax-free income of $15,000 a year. However, Doug and Kim didn't need the money, so they reinvested the interest earned from the municipal bonds. This money still found its way onto their tax return. Why did this happen?

It's because the interest earned from Doug and Kim's municipal bonds must be reported on their tax return, because that interest is included in their overall income calculation that determines how much of their Social Security is taxable. When their $15,000 in bond interest was factored in, Doug and Kim's income tax went from zero dollars to $3,000. Thus, their municipal bond interest was indirectly taxed at 20 percent. The municipal bond interest was taxed at zero, but that interest made other parts of the portfolio taxable, leading to the $3,000 tax. That's our tax code in action.

ROTH IRA DISTRIBUTIONS

In the fully taxable category, I mentioned there was an exception to tax-sheltered plans. Roth IRAs are the one tool in the tax code that is fully tax-free, provided you hold the funds in the account for five-years. Here's how the rules of Roth IRAs work: You deposit *after-tax* money in a Roth IRA and let it ride while it works for you gaining interest. After five years, all distributions from that Roth IRA and any subsequent Roth IRA will be completely tax-free. The five-year penalty is imposed only on the first contribution into the initial account. Once you pass the five-year benchmark, all Roth IRA money, even later contributions, are 100 percent tax-free and 100 percent available.

It gets even better. If you invested your money in a Roth IRA, once you turn fifty-nine and a half years old, you can start pulling money out on day one, and it's tax-free. Roth IRAs are fantastic tools because you can invest in anything you want inside the account and all growth and all distributions are completely tax-free.

DISTRIBUTION FROM PROPERLY DESIGNED LIFE INSURANCE

Corporations and banks have known about life insurance as an investment tool for years, but it has only recently become more mainstream and available to individuals. Anyone can put money in a properly designed life insurance policy and use it to generate income during retirement, and if structured correctly, that income is completely tax-free. I will discuss how to take advantage of these policies later in the book, but these tools are extremely complex and a full description of them is beyond the scope of this book. Be sure you're working with an advisor who's both an expert and a fiduciary if you are considering tools of this nature.

REVERSE MORTGAGES

Historically, hearing these two words conjured up negative feelings. However, in the midst of the 2008 financial collapse, the government cleaned up the reverse mortgage industry. Today, it is absolutely mainstream and 100 percent legitimate. That doesn't mean everyone should run out and get a reverse mortgage. It *does* mean that there is no reason to fear them. There are many situations where a reverse mortgage can be a fantastic tool when planning your retirement.

RETURN OF PRINCIPAL

Many people retire with a large sum of money sitting in savings due to a sale of a business, severance package, or maybe the proceeds from a real estate transaction when they downsized. For whatever reason, they've got a significant amount of money in the bank, and plan to take income from that account for living expenses in retirement. This is called *return of principal*. One could call it an income tool of sorts, but because someone is simply spending money they've already saved and not generating income from these accounts, per se, it is considered a tax-free source of income when it comes to tax planning.

SUMMARY

In this chapter, I have presented a look at some of the various ways different retirement income can be taxed. The complexities of our tax code dictate the need to carefully monitor your retirement financial plan, because mistakes can kick you into a higher tax bracket, the last thing you want to have happen. This is where the right professional advice is valuable, as a good Financial Advisor that knows the intricacies of taxation as it relates to retirement income streams can help you optimize your retirement dollars by avoiding unnecessary taxes.

For instance, if you are retired, and in your early sixties, it often makes sense to take advantage of the lower tax brackets and convert IRA dollars into Roth IRAs. This way, your required minimum distributions would be lower and you would be in a better tax bracket in your seventies and beyond. By paying a little bit of tax earlier, you can save a lot of tax later.

Unfortunately, retirees pay the IRS far more over time than necessary because they did not receive sound financial advice. People are so focused on today that they don't look at what the consequences of those actions will be tomorrow with regard to taxes.

There is one important point to consider as we discuss taxation. I can only offer a few guidelines with regard to tax planning in this book because every situation is different. The right Certified Financial Planner™ with a full knowledge of the tax code should know how different strategies would generate different taxation outcomes, but they do not replace a tax attorney as the final word on these issues.

CHAPTER 7

Putting It All
Together

So far in this section, we've discussed the components
in a retirement income plan, and we understand how
taxes work to some degree. This chapter will merge this
information as we explore two different allocation models
to build your plan: *General Income Model* and *Sequential
Income Model (SIPS)*. To close out the chapter, I will discuss
something called *Legacy Assets*, which is a completely different conversation in regards to your retirement income
plan, but one worth noting if you have extremely high
net worth.

GENERAL INCOME MODEL

This first allocation model places assets into four different
types of accounts. Going forward, let's assume you have $1

million saved for retirement and want to generate $3,000 a month or $36,000 a year in income. Everything that follows is based on that $1 million amount, so of course your results and allocation plan will need to be adjusted to match your real-world situation.

EMERGENCY ASSETS

Your first area to consider is how much you'll have set aside as *emergency assets*. During your working years, this should be equivalent to three to six months of income; however, in retirement, you need to set aside more for emergencies. If already retired, you should have twelve months of income set aside in emergency funds. For our example, that would be $36,000, or even up to $50,000 if you want to be prepared for unexpected emergencies.

Emergencies—as defined here—does not mean the house is on fire. Perhaps your roof needs significant repair or the furnace needs replacement. These are both huge outlays of money, and you may want to use cash instead of borrowing. The same goes for that new car purchase. In your working years, you may have been fine with monthly car payments, but in retirement, using cash instead may be a better option, depending on your circumstances. There could be a cruise in your future, or your children or grandchildren need money. Whatever the reason, while these expenses may not be true "emergencies," I find it's helpful for my clients to have a sufficient emergency fund in retirement.

Now that you've allocated some of your hypothetical $1 million in emergency funds, next we need to identify how to set aside the minimum of $3,000 a month for basic living expenses.

INCOME-PRODUCING ASSETS

In order to make your money work hard for you and produce money to live on, we need to allocate assets into an account called *Income-Producing Assets (IPA)*. We want to identify the smallest amount of money needed for this account to generate $3,000 a month over your lifetime. How is that accomplished exactly?

Let's say your Certified Financial Planner™ has found an IPA (or portfolio of IPAs) that will deliver 6 percent income for you. To have that account generate the $3,000 a month you'll need for basic living expenses, you'll need to allocate $600,000 of your money into the IPA. During retirement, the account that is tasked with producing these critical living expenses often is the largest portion of the General Income Model.

INFLATION PROTECTION ASSETS

We all know the importance of factoring inflation into our future financial projections. I'm sure you remember the 1970s and early 1980s when inflation was a serious problem.

Today, we live in a much different world regarding inflation, with a low rate hovering around 2 percent to 3 percent. While that number might not look like much, it's vital to recognize that you may live twenty to thirty years in retirement. Even in our current low inflation environment, inflation of any amount will still greatly affect your buying power. I tell my clients to put some percentage of their hypothetical $1 million into an account designated just for inflation protection. This might be a growth account, or it may hold more hard assets like gold, real estate, or other assets that tend to correlate closely to inflation such as *Treasury Inflation Bonds*. The purpose is to protect your assets and future income against inflation. You can use this account to generate the excess income you'll need down the road as inflation eats away at your buying power. Should the insane inflation rates of the 1970s ever return, you'll be ready.

EXTRAS ASSETS

Everyone reading this probably has a bucket list, if not on paper then certainly in their mind. Basically, anything outside of the emergency fund and inflation protection could fit in this category. Whether it's a long and expensive cruise like I mentioned previously, or the desire to fund your grandchildren's college education, having assets allocated for these "extras" is smart retirement planning.

The money for these "extras" accounts needs to be more conservatively invested. It can be growth-focused, but we'll call it conservative growth. Why? What if the market is down? You don't want to postpone a trip or put off a large purchase—that is just not good financial planning. If you have this money invested in order to get a decent return while protecting your downside exposure, you will have created a *hedge* that can keep your portfolio performing in any economy.

Even when the markets are not cooperating, having "extras" assets available means you can take advantage of these downturns. For example, the best time to book a vacation might be when the market is tanking, because this is when everyone else who planned wrong is left on the dock even though the cruise companies are offering deep discounts. You might get a better deal if you have cash available when markets are bad. Liquidity is key here, which positions yourself with more options to achieve the lifestyle you expect.

SEQUENTIAL INCOME MODEL (SIPS)

The next model is what I call a *Sequential Income Portfolio System*, which takes assets and identifies both income and timeframes. It helps determine *how* you decide to invest the money in all the accounts listed in the *General Income Model*. We'll use the same hypothetical $1 million example to explain this system. In this case, we decide to segregate the $36,000 a year for basic living expenses over certain timeframes: short-term, mid-term, and longer-term.

SHORT-TERM INCOME ASSETS

Since we already know that you'll need $36,000 in this example for the next few years, we'll simply put aside $72,000 in cash to handle the first two years of distributions. That will cover your *short-term income* needs. Often, we will simply put this money in your bank account.

MID-TERM INCOME ASSETS

Next, we will need to decide how much money to set aside for the next two to ten years. We need to generate $36,000 income each year for years three to ten, which equates to eight years of income, with the first two years already covered. How much money should we then set aside in a *mid-term* type of account that will guarantee that income? This is where we might use *bond ladders*.

For example, if you invest in a bond that matures in two years at a value of $36,000, you will have $36,000 cash at the end of that two-year period. That handles your income for year three. If you have another bond that matures at the end of year three for $36,000, that delivers the cash for year four, and so on. Every year, you'll have a bond that matures and you get another $36,000 dropped into cash in this mid-term account. That is an example of a bond ladder, and it can be an effective method to fund your basic living expenses.

Certainly, there are other ways to invest for this account than bond ladders. Again, this is where a Certified Financial Planner™ can help you evaluate your options.

LONGER-TERM ASSETS

To produce the *long-term income* you'll need in year eleven, and potentially for the next twenty years, we typically recommend using longer-term accounts. For example, you might use a type of *fixed annuity* with an *income rider*.

This is a tool generated by an insurance company, whereby if you give them X number of dollars today, they will guarantee that starting in year eleven, you can take that $36,000 as a withdrawal from your account each year for as long as you live. Typically, these are more guaranteed types of accounts earning interest over time.

One of the concerns people often have with annuities is that if they die, any remaining money in the account would go to the insurance company. While that is true with some types of annuities, it is not true with these. At your death, any remaining funds go to your named beneficiaries, just like any other account.

Another option for your long-term income is utilizing some type of growth portfolio. However, be aware that if the markets do not cooperate, you may not have enough money to make this plan work by the time year eleven rolls around.

It's important that you balance your goals with the different investment options and the risks associated with them to create a plan that works best for you.

Which of these approaches make the most sense for you? It depends on your circumstances. There are other models, but generally speaking, the two outlined here are the most frequently used and most effective for our clients.

LEGACY ASSETS

Before moving on to the next section covering what your retirement tax plan should look like, there is one area of your possible income plan left to detail, and that is what I call *legacy assets*. This category is only for those who have high net worth and want to make sure a certain portion of that wealth is passed along after they are gone.

To discuss legacy assets, I want to introduce you to my clients, "Gordon" and "Betty." Betty's father had passed away years earlier, but her mom recently passed and left her $350,000 of various assets in an investment account. This couple was doing fine financially and didn't need the money. In fact, they told me that they had no idea how they'd even spend it.

Betty said it was her mother's intention to set aside this money for the purpose of passing it on to her children when she died. But her mom never gave it to the kids because she never knew if she might need it down the road, and she didn't want to be a burden. Betty's mom earmarked that money for her children with the idea that she would never touch it except as a last resort. That's one example of a legacy account.

Another example is a client who came to me when her husband passed. She was holding a total portfolio of substantial assets worth $6 million. Based on her spending patterns, she would never spend more than $1 million, even if she needed expensive long-term healthcare. She was only spending $1,000 a month to live. We structured her portfolio so a large amount of the assets was placed in a legacy account for the sole purpose of going to her children.

Legacy accounts are also a wonderful way to increase your philanthropy. Without a need to use these funds for all of the expenses listed in this chapter, donating money to a favorite charity becomes an easy way to give back, do some good in the world, and maybe even change lives.

How legacy assets should be invested depends on the client's situation. However, if you're not looking at transitioning some of these legacy assets into life insurance, then you're missing out on opportunity, because nothing magnifies the worth of legacy assets more than properly designed life insurance policies.

Many people also combine their extras and legacy funds into one account. When everything necessary is taken care of, the account can be considered fun money and, if anything is left, upon death, it will be inherited by the children. These clients don't see this as separate monies, and are often heard saying, "Hey, look at me, I'm spending my children's inheritance!"

And is there anything wrong with that? Of course not! After all, if you don't spend your money, odds are good your children will.

In the next chapter, we'll discuss how taxes affect both models. As I have stated, it is vitally important that you work with a Certified Financial Planner™ who understands the tax impact on these various accounts. At the end of the day, every dollar you send to the IRS is a dollar you don't get to spend. In many respects, some would even call it a wasted dollar. Proper tax management, regardless of the model used, can make your money work far more efficiently, depending on the quality of your tax planning.

SECTION II

Tax Planning

CHAPTER 8

Paying Tax on the Money You Don't Use

Tax planning is one of the biggest areas where retirees are not getting the help and advice they need. About half of the people I talk to these days are doing their own taxes on TurboTax, and that's not tax planning—they're just putting the right numbers in the right boxes. The reality is that the overwhelming majority of all the big investment firms will not let their advisors discuss a client's taxes because it opens up liability. My office, however, does a tremendous amount of work helping retirees with their tax planning. My goal in the next few chapters is to shed light on how taxes affect retirees in certain common areas.

Many people think that the natural person to help with

their tax planning in retirement is their *Certified Public Accountant* (CPA), and that might be so. However, your Certified Financial Planner™ is often better positioned to oversee this important area of your retirement plan. To illustrate the point, let me introduce you to my friend Bob Keebler, a highly-regarded CPA.

I was talking with Bob one day when he told me that most CPAs can't afford to work with retirees—they really need to work only with businesses to cover employee costs and overhead. "I have to pay a kid fresh out of college $60,000 a year to prepare tax returns," Bob said. "If I have them only doing a simple tax return for a retiree, we can only charge that retiree about $300. That means they would need to do two hundred tax returns just for me to break even before anything going to overhead, insurance, and everything else. These kids can't do enough tax returns for someone who's retired to justify that salary. The reality is that there's no money for a CPA in tax planning for retirees, and as a result, we don't go there. For their tax planning, it has to be a Certified Financial Planner™, because you guys sit down across the table and do the investing for these folks, so you're the ones who have to do their tax planning these days."

BRENDAN AND THE SHOWER

We all know the tax code is ridiculously complicated, and

tax regulations change all the time. Therefore, it is important to make sure you're working with an advisor who is on top of these changes. There are many different ways a retirement plan can be structured, and some of them can be horrible when it comes to taxation.

To illustrate the general mistakes people often make when it comes to paying taxes in retirement and handing some of their money over to the IRS for no reason whatsoever, I'm going to share a story about my son, Brendan.

Brendan was sixteen years old at the time. My wife, Becky, and I were in the living room watching a television show. Brendan came home from work, ran upstairs to his bedroom, and turned on the shower. Moments later—like a typical teenage boy—he came pounding down the stairs, skipping two or three steps at a time. He went into the kitchen, opened the freezer, and pulled out the main staple of the teenage boy's diet, a frozen pizza. He set the pizza on the counter, turned on the oven, and proceeded to wait for the oven to preheat.

Meanwhile, as you may recall, he had turned on the shower upstairs, and it had been running this whole time. After about a minute, Becky turned around and said, "Brendan, what are you doing?" With a confused look on his face, he replied as any teenage boy would, "I'm making pizza."

"No! That's not what I'm talking about," Becky replied. "Why do you have the shower running upstairs if you're down here making pizza? Either go take the shower now, or run upstairs and turn off the water until you're ready to use it."

Why am I telling you a story about my goofy son in a chapter about taxes? Because I sit down every day in my office with people visiting us for the first time who are essentially doing what my son Brendan did: leaving the "shower" running even though they aren't using it.

I review tax returns all the time and see my clients' investment accounts structured in such a way that they are paying taxes every day, 24/7, all year long. The taxes are raining down on their investment accounts all day long just like that shower, even if they do not touch the money. This is a tragic waste. They are paying money to the IRS that they don't need to, and they'll never see it again.

The great news, though, is that I am about to turn that shower off and reduce your tax burden on money that is not being used.

PROPER OVERSIGHT—THE KEY TO CREATING TAX SAVINGS

Brendan's story illustrates the downside of what can

happen with after-tax accounts that are not properly structured. Every year, you can end up paying taxes on your growth, even when you aren't using the money. You may be reinvesting your earnings, and unnecessary taxation on that growth is an anchor that holds you back.

Let me explain with the following scenario. I had a couple come to me with their money in a combination of tax-deferred IRAs and after-tax accounts. They had a joint account with $500,000, which they inherited from both of their parents when they passed away. Let's call this couple "Charles" and "Debra."

Charles and Debra were both retired, and the $500,000 was money they weren't using. Yet, when I looked at their tax return, I identified that, in their situation, they were paying $5,613 to the IRS every single year because of the way that money was invested. Simple math tells us that if they kept that account as is for the next ten years, and they're paying the IRS $5,613 a year, they were going to end up handing over a total of $56,130 to the IRS over that ten-year period.

The problem was that they were working with people at a big Wall Street firm that clearly had no understanding of how taxes affect investments. We can't blame the firm, though, because tax planning is not their job. The investment counselors only focus on trying to make a good return. However, as wealth managers, Certified Financial Planners™ not only look at investments, but also income planning, tax planning, healthcare planning, and estate planning.

Charles and Debra were getting slammed with additional taxes they didn't need to pay. We were able to suggest some simple changes to their investment portfolio that you will read about in this chapter, and completely eliminated the $56,000 tax bill they would owe over the next ten years.

How much more in investment returns would they have had to earn to end up with an extra $56,000 in their pockets? Many times, smart tax planning can be as valuable, if not more so, than finding a hot money manager. And it's certainly easier to make happen.

It takes a keen understanding of how investments and the tax code correlate to accomplish this level of tax savings. If you are retired or close to retirement age, your investment advisor should be looking at your tax return to determine the tax impact of all your investments. Odds are they've never done this, because few advisors are willing to take the time, energy, and liability required to understand taxes and make recommendations. They only care about getting the highest return possible on your investments. And this is why many people experience the "shower tax" syndrome.

What follows are three solutions to illustrate how to start reducing your taxes on these taxable accounts.

TAX EFFICIENT TOOLS

The most common method we employ to manage tax liability are tax-efficient accounts and other investment tools that will work in your favor regarding taxes.

For example, with a fixed income plan, instead of using *corporate bonds* that generate taxable interest, choose *municipal bonds* where the interest is not taxable. This is a simple tool to start optimizing your retirement for tax efficiency, but many other tools are also available to deliver desired tax savings.

EXCHANGE-TRADED FUNDS (ETF)

Using *exchange-traded funds* (ETFs) instead of mutual funds is another method to make your portfolio more tax efficient.

ETFs are marketable securities similar to a stock that tracks an index such as the Dow Jones Industrial Average or S&P 500, a commodity, bonds, or other assets. But unlike mutual funds, ETFs trade like a common stock on a stock exchange and experience price changes throughout the day as they are bought and sold. ETFs normally have higher liquidity and lower fees than shares of a mutual fund.

There are many benefits that ETFs have over index funds, or mutual funds in general. When built correctly, they are more tax efficient, generating little to no tax as long as you are reinvesting the gains.

When it's time to actually use that money, an investor can cash out some of the positions and only owe tax at that time. And even then, typically you owe long-term capital gains tax, which is a lower amount than ordinary income tax.

Think of it like this; if it's now time to take that shower by withdrawing some of the funds, it's okay to turn the water back on and pay the taxes on the money you pulled out. It's even better if the taxes you pay are administered at a lower rate.

The good news is that when you cash out of an ETF, instead of owing tax at ordinary income rates, you'll now owe tax at a long-term capital gains tax rate, which is much lower. In other words, you still owe tax, but because you were wise about how your portfolio was designed, you will pay less.

MUTUAL FUNDS

Why not use *mutual funds?* One of the problems with mutual funds is they're generally not tax efficient. A typical mutual fund will represent probably two hundred stock positions within that fund, and every mutual fund has something called a *turnover ratio*. This ratio tells you how much buying and selling is happening within that fund during the year.

The average investor mistakenly believes they are long-term investors if they hold a particular mutual fund for twenty years. What they don't realize is that during those twenty years, the mutual fund's average holding period for any particular stock position is a year and a half at most. In reality, the investor is holding twenty years of a churning portfolio.

If the turnover ratio of that mutual fund is 50 percent or higher, half of those two hundred positions during the year have been sold and replaced. Therefore, over the course of a two-year period, almost every position has been sold and replaced with something else.

Managers of these mutual funds pay zero attention to the tax consequences of when they buy and sell. All they care about is trying to make the most money possible. If they sell a position only six months after buying it, all those gains are taxed at ordinary income tax rates.

But wait a minute, you say! The money in the fund wasn't spent—it was reinvested. This doesn't matter. You're paying tax anyway, because the fund manager sold your position.

All the buying and selling that goes on in mutual funds creates taxes, even though you aren't using any money. You're reinvesting, and the tax shower is still running. You're still paying taxes on money you're not using.

However, with ETFs, you don't have that same buying and selling going on inside the fund. Once a portfolio is built, it's left alone. There is no turnover. That's why ETFs are more tax efficient.

Every year at the end of January, if you own a mutual fund, you receive a Form 1099 that outlines all the taxable events that come directly to you as a result of the trading the fund managers have done that year. Markets go up and markets go down, but every year, you get a Form 1099, and every year, you're paying taxes. That's a problem with how mutual funds are constructed.

I recall a few years ago how many of my clients received a Form 1099 in January 2009, that outlined their taxable "gains" from 2008. They were shocked to learn that even though their mutual funds lost 30 percent, 40 percent, or more in that year, they still owed tax on "gains" from their funds!

How does this happen? You can thank our tax code. The bottom line is you don't become tax efficient in a portfolio by using mutual funds. ETFs however, are quite tax efficient. That's the big difference between these two types of accounts.

ANNUITIES—A DIFFERENT TOOL ALTOGETHER

Deferred annuities are contracts with insurance companies and are far different than a typical investment account with a big Wall Street firm like Schwab, Fidelity, or TD Ameritrade. Annuities come in many shapes and flavors—some are *fixed* annuities with a model that resembles a CD. There are also *variable* annuities that are sort of like holding mutual funds at an insurance company. There are *fixed-indexed* annuities that are hybrids of these other models. The purpose of this section is to not to go into all the different types of annuities, but to let you know that insurance companies enjoy considerably favorable tax treatment from the tax code.

TAX DEFERRAL

By investing your money in after-tax accounts with an insurance company such as an annuity, you can enjoy the benefits of tax deferral. You won't pay tax on the gains; you only pay tax when you make withdrawals. From a tax perspective, annuities work just like other tax-deferred accounts. The only difference is there are no required minimum distributions, which means you never have to make withdrawals.

One reason people might use an annuity is that some provide guaranteed income in the future. Other annuities are structured to provide long-term care benefits. These are attractive options to place portions of your money. As part of an overall retirement portfolio, annuities do make sense when set up correctly.

DISADVANTAGES

The disadvantage of annuities when compared to a portfolio invested in ETFs is that when you're ready to withdraw money from an annuity, any earnings come out first using a method called *Last In, First Out (LIFO)*. That means earnings come first and are taxed as ordinary income at the higher tax rates. The principal comes out second and is called a return of principal, and is tax-free. There are many complexities to setting up annuities, which is why a Certified Financial Planner™ who is skilled at building retirement plans will be of great value.

LIFE INSURANCE—A DIFFERENT APPROACH

The third path to reduce tax on money that is reinvested is something that you don't see often, and yet, when set up correctly, it can be one of the most powerful investment tools you can use. You can transition after-tax money into a properly designed *life insurance program* where it can provide tax-free growth and tax-free distributions. Some people call these policies *Super Roth IRAs*.

As mentioned previously, insurance companies enjoy a favorable relationship with the tax code for reasons that go all the way back to the Great Depression when they were one of the very few safe havens for the public to put their money. Those deeds have not been forgotten.

You might be retired or nearing retirement and think you don't need life insurance—you're still young and living a vibrant lifestyle in your "Go-Go" years. Most people only view life insurance as something that provides a death benefit after you pass, but when structured properly, these programs can be extremely helpful to your portfolio regardless of your age or retirement status.

Let's break this down, shall we?

THE TAX-FREE BENEFITS OF LIFE INSURANCE ARE ENORMOUS

Normally, you have to leave money placed in this type of life insurance program untouched for a five-year period, and you cannot invest it all in one lump sum, so that is somewhat of a disadvantage. You have to spread your deposits into an account like this over a period of time in order for this scenario to work. Once all these accounts have been set up, though, after five years, all growth and all distributions are tax-free. In addition, you'll have a death benefit that is larger than your account value, which is also tax-free. When a long-term healthcare benefit is also linked to the death benefit, it is tax-free as well.

Here's the kicker, the key part of this scenario most people have never considered. If you do need the money, you can use these programs to generate tax-free income for your retirement. Let me repeat this: everything about this type of account is tax-free.

People who retire in today's environment typically have a lot of money in IRAs, 401(k)s or 403(b)s. When money is withdrawn from those accounts, it is taxed. We'll talk about this later in the book, but it is imperative for you to understand that if you die and you've left your surviving spouse money in an IRA or 401(k), every dollar that your spouse withdraws is taxable.

Also, your spouse is then considered a single taxpayer and will probably be thrust into a higher tax bracket. Essentially, you've not only left your grieving widow or widower a big taxable IRA account, but now they are also in a higher tax bracket for the rest of their lives. That is not the kind of parting gift you want to give them at this transitional period in their lives.

I'm sure you would agree this is probably not the best plan. What if, on the other hand, you had tax-free money coming from a life insurance program at this juncture? You die—sorry about that—and the death benefit is paid out, tax-free. It's a big check at a welcome time, and that money can be leveraged to help your surviving spouse and their retirement tax obligations.

Your surviving spouse was lucky that you also left him or her a traditional tax-deferred IRA, which can now be converted to a Roth IRA, with the life insurance money used to pay the tax generated by the conversion. Your spouse will then hold a tax-free Roth IRA, *with access to tax-free money for the rest of their lives.* This is a benefit of a life insurance program that is often overlooked, and it's a nice option to have available.

Typically, these types of programs fall under the category of *maximum-funded universal life.* Be mindful that not all are created equal. Again, do your due diligence and work with a professional who is well versed in these tools.

DISADVANTAGES

Although properly designed life insurance programs are

great investment tools, there are a few disadvantages to using insurance this specific way.

Costs

It is life insurance after all, so there are costs to the coverage. Even though you're not paying taxes, you are paying the insurance company what is called *mortality expense*. If the program has been structured properly, these costs will be kept at a minimum. Typically, these expenses are front-loaded, which means they tend to be higher in the early years and less costly down the road.

Will You Qualify?

You actually have to qualify to get life insurance, and not everyone is insurable. Many people nearing retirement are concerned that life insurance will cost a lot of money even if they do qualify. The good news is that since people are living longer, insurance costs have been reduced dramatically.

On the plus side, these costs are not nearly as high as you might think. Most people in their "Go-Go" years are still insurable unless they've suffered from major health problems. What might disqualify you from life insurance are the big, life-threatening conditions like heart conditions or cancer. However, if you had a condition or disease, were treated, and it's been five or ten years, you should still qualify. On the other hand, if you have diabetes and take insulin, that will most likely disqualify you to get life insurance.

Not All Insurance Agents Are Created Equal

This could be your biggest roadblock to obtaining a properly designed life insurance program like this. Few insurance agents are familiar with these types of programs, and most insurance agents are simply selling the death benefits. In these types of programs, though, the death benefit is almost irrelevant. The goal is to deposit as much cash as you can into these accounts and make them all tax-free. In addition, you want the death benefit to be as small as legally possible to reap the maximum tax benefits on your invested cash.

When shopping for life insurance, you must remember that insurance agents may understand this kind of program, but they'll never bring it up in their pitch. Why? Because that agent gets paid the least amount of commission possible for that contract if it is created in this manner. This is why you want to work with a Certified Financial Planner™ acting as a fiduciary that understands the complex inner workings of these programs. A fiduciary will make sure decisions serve their client's best interest, not those of the insurance company or agent.

People often ask me if they should get rid of their life insurance as they enter into retirement because they think they don't need it anymore. This fires me up, because the institution that pushes this idea the most is actually the insurance industry. They want you to get rid of your insurance when you retire because you are more likely to die after you retire. *If they can get out from underneath the contract before you die, they don't have to pay the death benefit.* This is why insurance companies encourage retirees to cash in their insurance before they pass on, thus avoiding payouts of the death benefits.

The day you die, your life insurance is probably the most valuable asset you have, and it's the most tax-efficient way to pass assets to a surviving spouse or children. Take proper precautions to construct these programs to your benefit, and your next of kin will thank you some day.

WHAT ABOUT MUNICIPAL BONDS?

The advantages to municipal bonds are that the interest is tax-free, and your principal is well protected. The disadvantages are that interest rates today are low, with a ten-year municipal bond at 1.9 percent as of this writing. In the grand scheme of your overall retirement portfolio, 1.9 percent is barely worth considering. We'll talk about that in the next chapter.

CHOOSING THE RIGHT ADVISOR IS KEY

By now, it's probably become apparent that there are a multitude of options available in constructing your retirement financial plan that you are not aware of because no one has ever taken the time to introduce you to them. You also may have realized that some of your current choices are hurting your financial future. The biggest problem with the tax code is that you just don't know what you don't know. Finding the right Financial Advisor is critical—someone who truly understands these areas, the tax code as it applies to retirement planning, and how different investments affect your retirement.

The right advisor is one that will save you a lot of money on taxes, because taxes impact your retirement finances in a big way. What kind of Financial Advisor ignores that impact on your life? If you don't have someone considering the implications of your retirement plan as it relates to taxes, you don't really have an advisor, even if you think you do. Maybe it's time to ask yourself if they are acting in *your* best interests, or that of some other entity.

The answer to that question might be a bit revealing.

CHAPTER 9

Taxes and Social Security

Can we be honest with each other? Social Security and Medicare are basically the two biggest Ponzi schemes in the world. A Ponzi scheme involves paying off existing investors with new investor money, rather than money earned on the investments. That's exactly how both Social Security and Medicare are set up.

In the 1930s, Franklin D. Roosevelt gave birth to Social Security with the advent of the New Deal. The concept was pretty simple. You had to be sixty-five to receive Social Security benefits. The average life expectancy of an American citizen at the time was sixty-two, which was considered "old age" back then. Americans were told they would be taxed as their money went into the Social Security system; however, when they received benefits at age sixty-five, they would not be taxed, as that would be considered double taxation.

It worked this way for many, many years. However, in the 1980s, actuaries started to recognize that people were living longer. In addition, the age was dropped to sixty-two, allowing people to begin taking benefits earlier, albeit at lower amounts. You could receive more money, however, if you waited to start taking your Social Security benefits. For these reasons, more people were collecting more money on Social Security than anyone had ever imagined. The number of workers paying into the system compared to how many were drawing Social Security benefits became unbalanced.

MODIFIED ADJUSTED GROSS INCOME

To remedy this, in the early 1980s after conducting "means testing," the IRS implemented a calculation called *modified adjusted gross income (MAGI)*. This factor is determined through a calculation adding 50 percent of your Social Security income to all other income, and it essentially let the IRS know if you are considered wealthy or poor. If you were married and your MAGI exceeded $32,000, then you were placed in the wealthy category, and if you earned less than $32,000, you were considered poor, thus no tax on Social Security. If you were single, the annual MAGI limit was $25,000. This was a successful move for

Social Security because, in those days, few retirees had $32,000 of annual income.

Let's look at an example of how this MAGI calculation works.

Let's imagine that you had $36,000 a year of Social Security income as a married couple and were also taking an additional $24,000 out of your IRA. Half of Social Security income would be $18,000. Your other income is the $24,000 from your IRA, so $18,000 plus $24,000 gives you $42,000 of MAGI. You have exceeded the $32,000 threshold, so half of your Social Security is considered part of your taxable income.

Social Security Benefits Worksheet—Lines 20a and 20b

Keep for Your Records

Before you begin:
- ✓ Complete Form 1040, lines 21 and 23 through 32, if they apply to you.
- ✓ Figure any write-in adjustments to be entered on the dotted line next to line 36 (see the instructions for line 36).
- ✓ If you are married filing separately and you lived apart from your spouse for all of 2016, enter "D" to the right of the word "benefits" on line 20a. If you do not, you may get a math error notice from the IRS.
- ✓ Be sure you have read the **Exception** in the line 20a and 20b instructions to see if you can use this worksheet instead of a publication to find out if any of your benefits are taxable.

1. Enter the total amount from **box 5 of all** your **Forms SSA-1099** and **Forms RRB-1099**. Also, enter this amount on Form 1040, line 20a .... **1.** _____

2. Multiply line 1 by 50% (0.50) .... **2.** _____

3. Combine the amounts from Form 1040, lines 7, 8a, 9a, 10 through 14, 15b, 16b, 17 through 19, and 21 .... **3.** _____

4. Enter the amount, if any, from Form 1040, line 8b .... **4.** _____

5. Combine lines 2, 3, and 4 .... **5.** _____

6. Enter the total of the amounts from Form 1040, lines 23 through 32, plus any write-in adjustments you entered on the dotted line next to line 36 .... **6.** _____

7. Is the amount on line 6 less than the amount on line 5?

   ☐ **No.** ⊘ None of your social security benefits are taxable. Enter -0- on Form 1040, line 20b.

   ☐ **Yes.** Subtract line 6 from line 5 .... **7.** _____

8. If you are:
   - Married filing jointly, enter $32,000
   - Single, head of household, qualifying widow(er), or married filing separately and you **lived apart** from your spouse for all of 2016, enter $25,000
   - Married filing separately and you lived with your spouse at any time in 2016, skip lines 8 through 15; multiply line 7 by 85% (0.85) and enter the result on line 16. Then, go to line 17
   .... **8.** _____

9. Is the amount on line 8 less than the amount on line 7?

   ☐ **No.** ⊘ None of your social security benefits are taxable. Enter -0- on Form 1040, line 20b. If you are married filing separately and you **lived apart** from your spouse for all of 2016, be sure you entered "D" to the right of the word "benefits" on line 20a.

   ☐ **Yes.** Subtract line 8 from line 7 .... **9.** _____

10. Enter: $12,000 if married filing jointly; $9,000 if single, head of household, qualifying widow(er), or married filing separately and you **lived apart** from your spouse for all of 2016 .... **10.** _____

11. Subtract line 10 from line 9. If zero or less, enter -0- .... **11.** _____

12. Enter the **smaller** of line 9 or line 10 .... **12.** _____

13. Enter one-half of line 12 .... **13.** _____

14. Enter the **smaller** of line 2 or line 13 .... **14.** _____

15. Multiply line 11 by 85% (0.85). If line 11 is zero, enter -0- .... **15.** _____

16. Add lines 14 and 15 .... **16.** _____

17. Multiply line 1 by 85% (0.85) .... **17.** _____

18. **Taxable social security benefits.** Enter the **smaller** of line 16 or line 17. Also enter this amount on Form 1040, line 20b .... **18.** _____

TIP *If any of your benefits are taxable for 2016 **and** they include a lump-sum benefit payment that was for an earlier year, you may be able to reduce the taxable amount. See Lump-Sum Election in Pub. 915 for details.*

CHAPTER 10

Qualified
Retirement Plans

To begin this chapter, I want to introduce you to "Farmer Brown" who owns a farm comprised of hundreds of acres. This story will help to set the tone here and allow you to better understand the next few chapters of the book.

Every year, Farmer Brown has a choice to make. He can choose to pay a tax on the seeds he plants in the spring, or wait and pay the tax on the huge crop he harvests in the fall. Which tax would *you* pay if given this choice? Would you pay tax on the seed (the smaller amount, thus a smaller tax), or the harvest (the larger amount, thus a larger tax)?

Obviously, Farmer Brown will want to pay tax on the seed as it represents less tax.

Farmer Brown's fictional story is just like retirement finances. You can choose to pay tax now on some of your money (Roth IRA approach), or wait for years and pay substantially more tax on that same money after it has the chance to grow (401k, 403b, 457, IRA approach).

When given the option as presented, I am sure both you and Farmer Brown would choose to pay on the seeds and not on the harvest.

We are facing a much larger challenge than we've had in the past with regard to the various retirement plans most retirees have in place. When my father retired in 2000, his pension and Social Security covered all of his basic income needs, and his 401(k) retirement plan was extra money.

The problem we are facing now is that very few people retiring today have pensions, because as previously stated, most companies in the 1980s and 1990s moved away from pensions and started pushing 401(k)s. With 401(k)s, companies were contributing money in these accounts as *company matches*. They made it easy for employees to make direct, automatic deductions from their paychecks.

The result is that people retiring today usually rely on their Social Security plus retirement plan distributions for their retirement income. Those retirement plans have grown larger than they've ever been, and it is not uncommon in my office to see $1 million-plus retirement plans.

While you're working, a retirement plan is an outstanding tax shelter. However, the instant you retire, that wonderful tax shelter becomes the absolutely worst asset you own from a tax perspective. It is important to understand why.

Every dollar that comes out is going to be taxed at whatever your highest current tax bracket is. If you're in the 25 percent tax bracket, you're going to pay 25 percent tax on that distribution. Additionally, every dollar that comes out has the potential to put you in a higher tax bracket, and goes into your MAGI calculation. Therefore, distributions from a tax-deferred account often increase the tax you end up paying on your Social Security income as well.

Leaving a tax-deferred account like an IRA to your surviving spouse is the absolute worst thing you could do from a tax perspective. Why? When you were married, you filed taxes jointly, and those are the lowest tax brackets. If you're single, though, you are subject to the worst tax brackets. When you pass away, your surviving spouse instantly becomes a single taxpayer. If you leave them a retirement plan as an inheritance, you have essentially left a fully taxable account to someone who has now shifted into the highest tax brackets in the tax code. This is obviously not a good plan.

IT'S NEVER TOO LATE FOR AN EXIT STRATEGY

Once you've retired, there is absolutely zero reason in today's world to leave any dollars in any *Qualified Retirement Plans (QFPs)*—401(k), 403(b), 457, etc. You can transfer money from these plans straight to an individual IRA or multiple IRAs with a tax-free, direct rollover. This can avoid confusion that can cause missteps with some expensive tax implications.

REQUIRED MINIMUM DISTRIBUTIONS

One of the biggest reasons to move your money into IRAs is because, once you turn seventy and a half, you must start taking required minimum distributions every single year.

Use this worksheet to figure this year's required withdrawal for your traditional IRA UNLESS your spouse[1] is the sole beneficiary of your IRA and he or she is more than 10 years younger than you.

Deadline for receiving required minimum distribution:
- Year you turn age 70 ½ - by April 1 of the following year
- All subsequent years - by December 31 of that year

1. IRA balance[2] on December 31 of the previous year. $_____

2. Distribution period from the table below for your age on your   _____
   birthday this year.

3. Line 1 divided by number entered on line 2. This is your required $_____
   minimum distribution for this year from this IRA.

4. Repeat steps 1 through 3 for each of your IRAs.

Table III (Uniform Lifetime)

Age	Distribution Period	Age	Distribution Period	Age	Distribution Period	Age	Distribution Period
70	27.4	82	17.1	94	9.1	106	4.2
71	26.5	83	16.3	95	8.6	107	3.9
72	25.6	84	15.5	96	8.1	108	3.7
73	24.7	85	14.8	97	7.6	109	3.4
74	23.8	86	14.1	98	7.1	110	3.1
75	22.9	87	13.4	99	6.7	111	2.9
76	22.0	88	12.7	100	6.3	112	2.6
77	21.2	89	12.0	101	5.9	113	2.4
78	20.3	90	11.4	102	5.5	114	2.1
79	19.5	91	10.8	103	5.2	115 and over	1.9
80	18.7	92	10.2	104	4.9		
81	17.9	93	9.6	105	4.5		

Once you determine a separate required minimum distribution from each of your traditional IRAs, you can total these minimum amounts and take them from any one or more of your traditional IRAs.

CHAPTER 11

IRA Exit Strategies: Roth Conversions

A large number of people have heard the phrase *Roth IRA* but don't have a clear understanding of what they are. Similar to our Farmer Brown story, with a Roth IRA, you are essentially paying tax on the seed instead of the harvest. A Roth IRA is funded with after-tax dollars, or money you've already paid tax on. Once the money is in the account, however, it grows tax-free and is distributed tax-free.

There are certain rules that you need to follow, but if you're over the age of fifty-nine and a half, many of them don't apply, except in rare circumstances. There are also no required distributions on Roth IRAs. You have complete freedom. When you die, any money left in this type of IRA goes to your beneficiaries tax-free. If you are married, your spouse can take it over and the same rules apply; it's tax-free for the rest of their life.

If it goes to children, grandchildren, other family or friends, it is still tax-free; however, a non-spouse beneficiary does have to take required distributions, where a spouse does not. When you do you take distributions, as we've mentioned before, it does not show up anywhere on your tax return. This is by far the best account to hold money. Outside of life insurance, a Roth IRA is as good as it gets in the tax code.

In order to contribute money to a Roth IRA, you must first have earned income, which simply means that you have wages. Second, if you make too much money you cannot contribute. Typically, this is around $135,000 per year for a single tax filer, and $200,000 per year for a married filer. If you make more than that, you cannot add money to a Roth IRA.

If you don't have earned income and cannot contribute to a Roth IRA, what many people do, is take an existing IRA and convert portions of that into a Roth IRA. You can convert the entire amount if you wish; however, there are costs to consider because you'll have to pay income tax on the amount you convert.

Here's an example. You have an IRA with $500,000 and

decide you want to convert $100,000 from an IRA to a Roth IRA this year. You will owe tax on $100,000 of income for the year on the IRA you converted. Where are you going to get the money to pay the tax? Ideally, you will have money set aside in savings or after-tax accounts. If you don't, the good news is if you're over the age of fifty-nine and a half, you can pull that money immediately out of your Roth IRA, tax-free, and use it to pay the tax. There are many ways to access the money needed for taxes.

Be aware though that converting IRAs to Roth IRAs is not something to take lightly. You should sit down with your Financial Advisor or accountant every single year and have a conversation. You need to decide to what degree would it be wise to make a Roth conversion. This is a year-by-year discussion.

One of my clients has $1,000,000 in his IRA and they asked us to convert only $30,000 or $40,000 of it each year to their Roth IRA while his tax rate was around 20 percent. The client thought it was great that if he kept it up for ten years, he would have converted $300,000 to $400,000 of his IRA at a pretty cheap tax rate.

The number one misconception I hear is, "I've thought about doing a Roth conversion, but my advisor tells me I'm too old." The *only* question you have to ask is: do you expect your IRA to grow over time for the rest of your life or not? Because if it's going to grow, guess what? You or someone else is going to pay tax on even more money at some point. If your IRA is worth $500,000 today and you do a Roth conversion, you pay tax on $500,000. But if that IRA grows to $700,000 over the next five to eight years, now you owe tax on $700,000. What would you rather pay tax on, $500,000 or $700,000?

This concept of "I'm too old" is silly. Somebody's going to pay tax. It might be you or your family members, but somebody is paying that tax.

The second big problem or misconception is the lack of objective perspective. Not a week goes by that I don't talk to someone who says they thought about doing a Roth conversion and went onto Vanguard®, Schwab, or Fidelity's website. They all offer Roth conversion calculators. They say that based upon their calculations, they don't see any benefit to do a Roth conversion. Even worse, they may have consulted with their Financial Advisor and both agreed that it didn't make sense to convert.

Consider the source. Imagine you have a $500,000 IRA. The first thing you need to recognize is it's not all your money. You have a partner in this IRA, called the IRS. If you were to cash that IRA out all in one lump sum, you'd probably get about $300,000 to $350,000. The IRS would get the rest. If you do a Roth conversion on the $500,000

IRA, you're going to be left with $300,000 to $350,000 after taxes are paid. *Making the Roth conversion is basically buying out your silent partner called the IRS.*

If you were a large institutional broker or a Financial Advisor, would you ever want your client to do a Roth conversion and buy out their partner, the IRS? The answer is no. Right now, on that $500,000 IRA, the institution or advisor tasked with managing your account is getting paid on managing the full $500,000. They're getting paid on managing your money, and they're also getting paid the portion of the money that will eventually go to the IRS as taxes.

On the other hand, if you convert that IRA to a Roth IRA, suddenly they won't get paid on the IRS's portion any longer because the taxes have been paid and the IRS is out of the picture. They will only get paid on your remaining portion. Those institutions, or your Financial Advisor, get paid less on the remaining funds when you do a Roth conversion. You can see that it is never in their best interest to tell you to do a conversion. As a result, every single online calculator for determining whether a Roth IRA conversion is a smart move for you is designed specifically to give you the answer that no, you should not convert.

None of these Financial Advisors or institutional brokers takes into account the fact that you don't have required minimum distributions anymore. This means that not only do you save tax on your IRA, but you also may pay less tax on your Social Security in your later years if you do not need to withdraw funds as a distribution. Another thing that these managers do not fit into the equation is that if your income gets too high due to required distributions considered as income, Medicare has penalties in the form of extra premiums that you pay. If you do a Roth conversion, you're not paying any of those penalties.

None of those online calculators include those points. Nor do they include the fact that when you die, if you are leaving your spouse money from an IRA, those funds will be taxed at the higher, single tax bracket because now your spouse is a widow and no longer married. Again, advantage goes to the Roth IRA and its tax-free benefits.

Here's another way to look at this issue.

Let's say our friend "Don" has an IRA worth $500,000. Don gets his statement, and it says, "Don's IRA" with a balance of $500,000. Does Don really have $500,000?

The answer is, of course, no. What is something worth? An item is worth the amount of cash you can put in your pocket after all expenses when you sell it to another party.

How much cash can Don put in his pocket when he sells

out of his $500,000 IRA after all expenses? The answer is around $300,000 to $350,000 after taxes have been paid. If that is the case, what is his $500,000 IRA (or 401(k) or 403(b), etc.) really worth? Between $300,000 to $350,000.

For comparison, let's imagine that Don received a statement from his Roth IRA account with a balance of $500,000. The fund has the exact same mutual funds and exact same positions that his IRA had in the previous example. When Don cashes the Roth IRA out, he gets to put the full $500,000 in his pocket because the taxes have already been paid.

When you see your balance on your IRA statement, you need to recognize that it is *not all your money*. The account balance you see is misleading, as the expenses (taxes) are not yet taken out. It's like saying you have a house worth $500,000, but you ignore the fact that you still have $150,000 mortgaged on it. What would that house be worth to you if you sold it? About $350,000, as you need to deduct the mortgage. An IRA is the same.

Why is this? Because only a portion of the money in an IRA is actually yours. To be perfectly correct, that statement should have been titled, "Don and the IRS's IRA," because a sizable portion of it will eventually go to taxes. When you do a Roth conversion, what you're really doing is basically saying you want the IRS out of your account—in essence, you are buying your silent partner out.

The power of a Roth IRA, on the other hand, is that the number you see is the number you truly have. On top of that, you are immunized against any tax changes in the future, along with no required distributions, etc. It's just part of the deal of owning a Roth.

For all of these reasons, it is almost *always* a good idea to kick the IRS out of your account.

For the large institutional brokers or your Financial Advisor, it is always against their best interest to handle Roth conversions for you. What's good for *you* is not good for *them*. Bottom line is that it's really hard to get any of the online Roth IRA conversion calculators to say yes. They are not objective, and are programmed to generate data that sides with the institution or advisors that present them on their website.

When viewed through this lens, it is easy to see that there are plenty of benefits to a Roth IRA conversion when all aspects are considered. As with everything in this book, if your Certified Financial Planner™ has a full tool kit to effectively manage your retirement portfolio, they will approach every decision with what is best for *you*.

How your decisions will affect brokers, institutions, or fund managers should never matter.

CHAPTER 12

IRA Exit Strategies: QRP Rollout

In the last chapter, we talked about Roth IRAs sitting at the top of the tax code as one of the best methods to receive tax-free funds in retirement. That is until you consider a *Qualified Retirement Plan rollout* (QRP rollout), which is an even more tax-efficient vehicle based on *maximum-funded cash value life insurance.*

Whenever I talk about life insurance, people are somewhat taken aback at first. They might have had life insurance when they were younger because they had children, a mortgage, etc. This is a far different investment tool. I'm talking about utilizing life insurance the way that banks and big corporations—BIG buyers of life insurance—use it. They understand how advantageous life insurance can be with regard to taxes.

Normally, when we think about life insurance, we calculate how big of a death benefit we get in exchange for our premiums. But a contract for a maximum-funded cash value life insurance policy literally flips this concept on its head.

The banks and corporations obviously don't want the death benefit; they only want to invest tax-free without any restrictions on how much money they can invest. For these big institutional life insurance buyers, they strive to make the death benefit as small as possible.

In order to structure this so that everything's tax-free, you cannot take an IRA and deposit all your money into a maximum-funded life insurance policy all at once. You have to roll it out over a five-year period—the minimum time allowed by the IRS. A QRP rollout takes a portion of an IRA and it rolls it into these specially designed life insurance contracts over a five-year period. Essentially what you've done is similar to a Roth conversion, only now it's called life insurance.

The difference is that life insurance still has a death benefit, even if it's small. When you do a Roth conversion, you pay the tax on that conversion and never recoup that money. With life insurance, you also pay tax on the rollout; however. this is temporary. When you die, the insurance company pays back your family all those taxes and more, tax-free, via the death benefit.

In addition to that, most of these insurance plans also have long-term care benefits if you need it later on. We won't go into this is in great detail, but it is important to understand these benefits are available.

If we take our $500,000 IRA from our example in the last chapter, we could convert $100,000 a year for five years into a Roth IRA. There are many benefits for doing that. By using life insurance, you're doing the exact same thing— converting your IRA status to tax-free status over the next five years. Instead of using a Roth, you are using life insurance because of all the additional benefits that accrue.

One disadvantage to this approach is you still have to pay tax as you make the transition, although that money is recouped later via the death benefit. A bigger disadvantage is you might not be able to qualify for life insurance. Once people reach age sixty to seventy, they've usually had some health issues along the way, and life insurance companies might reject their applications, as I explained earlier in the book. The good news is that you don't have to be a marathon runner; you just have to be insurable.

In addition, there are costs to the insurance coverage. That's one of the reasons to keep the death benefit as low as possible. You want to make sure you understand what those costs are and how they impact the growth of your money over time.

One final disadvantage is typically you are not permitted to move more than 30 percent of your IRA into a maximum-funded cash value life insurance strategy like this. That means if you have a $1 million IRA, you will only have $300,000 to work with. Again, if you're going to consider this type of strategy you need to be working with an expert in this environment. That expert will not typically be your life insurance salesman, because this type of insurance delivers the smallest commission possible to an insurance agent. As a result, few agents want to consider it.

Please note that these types of life insurance products can often be called *indexed universal life, variable universal life,* or *maximum-funded indexed universal life.* While the name may change, they do represent another additional opportunity to exit a tax-deferred IRA in a more tax-efficient manner.

CHAPTER 13

Tax Planning for People Who Don't Need the Money

If you are fortunate enough to possess IRA money that you don't really need, you might want to know how to make it as large as possible on a guaranteed basis.

This is where *insurance arbitrage* might come into play. You could take your IRA to insurance company A and say, "I would like to *annuitize* my IRA." This is the exact phrase. Essentially, you're handing that contract to an insurance company and telling them to keep the lump sum as long as they pay you income for the rest of your life.

Then, since you do not need the money, you would take your income checks from that first insurance company, pay the tax, and go to insurance company B with the balance. It has to be a different company for tax reasons. You tell insurance company B you're getting these premiums for the rest of your life and you want to know what is the largest *joint survivorship death benefit* they offer for that same premium amount. In other words, what is the death benefit paid out after you and your spouse are both gone. The following scenario is common.

Insurance company A says, "You have $1 million in your IRA, so we'll pay you $70,000 a year for the rest of both your lives." You have to pay tax on that $70,000, so you'll have about $50,000 a year left over.

Next, you take the $50,000 to insurance company B and say, "I want to know how big a death benefit I can get for this $50,000 annual premium." They will probably respond with a number in the neighborhood of $3 million.

Therefore, if you died with that $1 million in your IRA account, that is taxable money going to your children with a net value of $600,000 to $700,000. However, in the scenario outlined above, your kids would get $3 million tax-free. This is insurance arbitrage at work.

This is a simple way to leverage insurance companies with a taxable IRA that has required distributions. It works best if you don't need the money. You can leverage it to create maximum value for your children, grandchildren, or your charity in the most tax-efficient way possible.

There was a time when I only worked with people that didn't need income, so we took advantage of this strategy quite often. However, more people need income today, so this insurance arbitrage strategy doesn't work for everyone. But when we can find the right fit, it's a clever tool to use.

SECTION III

Healthcare Plan

CHAPTER 14

Long-Term Care

In this section, we'll discuss an important topic that nobody wants to talk about: long-term care. Unless something has happened recently to a friend or family member that required significant hospitalization or rehabilitation, people usually avoid discussions about this type of care.

According to several studies, there is about a 70 percent probability that you will need long-term care assistance at some point in your life. Because health insurance and Medicare don't cover long-term care, these expenses are all out-of-pocket and can be expensive. If you ignore this "elephant in the room," you do so at your own peril.

The extreme costs of long-term care conjures up fear in many people who for some reason have neglected to arrange for this critical care that usually happens well into your "No-Go" years, but can happen sooner. I asked one client recently about his long-term care plans. He said, "Well, I have a gun in my dresser drawer, and I know how to use it." He was joking of course, so I replied, "That may be true, but by then, you'll have Alzheimer's and you won't remember that you own a gun or even remember where you put it!"

All joking aside, this is a real concern. If and when there is a health crisis, the expense for care is probably more than you might expect. Depending on where you live, it could be $7,000 or more a month for a nursing home or a room in an assisted living center. And that is today. The costs continue to skyrocket every year. If you ignore the inevitable like so many retirees often do, you can get caught in a financial situation with a serious need for care and no money to pay for it.

A great online resource that calculates long-term care costs where you live is Genworth's online Annual Cost of Care Survey found at www.genworth.com. MetLife also has an online survey identifying costs in your area for home care, different types of assisted living, and costs of private versus semi-private nursing homes.

Geography dictates the cost of long-term care, and some states are more expensive than others. If you live on the west coast in California, Oregon, Washington, or on the East Coast, all the way from Massachusetts south to Florida, this type of care can cost up to $15,000 a month. In the middle of the country, it is still a significant cost, but not as much.

You need to be aware of these expenses and factor them into your retirement planning. It's important to note that health insurance premiums and healthcare costs are increasing at a rate significantly faster than inflation. A lot of retired married couples don't consider these expenses and end up self-insuring, which means they pay for the care themselves. This sets up a horrible financial scenario that can wipe out your retirement savings.

For example, say the husband has a stroke and cannot move one side of his body. He now needs help eating, bathing, dressing, and going to the bathroom. Now imagine that his wife is seventy-five or eighty years old, trying to lift her husband in and out of a bathtub. This is physically next-to-impossible for her to do, so she has to hire someone to help.

Medicare and health insurance won't pay for that. The health insurance industry, Medicare included, is designed to pay for what are called *acute incidents*. Something happens, you go to the doctor, and you get better. Long-term care is for *degenerative conditions* where you don't get better and just keep getting worse. Knowing the difference between the two is vital to understanding the potential expenses of long-term care.

Home-based healthcare usually costs about half of the price of going to a skilled nursing center. If a bed in this type of facility in your state costs $7,000 a month, hiring someone to come to your home is approximately $3,500 per month, or $42,000 a year. In the case above, if this gentleman gets worse, his wife may have to move him to an assisted living facility and eventually into a nursing home. If this lasts for three or four years, before long, they've blown through a substantial amount of money. Healthcare can easily cost as much as $200,000 to $400,000 when something of this nature happens.

And remember, these are today's numbers. It will cost a lot more in the future, due to inflation.

If the husband's care in this example eats through as much as $400,000, how much of this couple's nest egg is left over for his wife when he dies? On average, wives outlive their husbands by about seven years, and if this happens, where is she going to get money for her own care? It is common for people to spend their entire life savings on a healthcare incident with the first spouse, leaving the surviving spouse with next to nothing when the first spouse passes away. That's something every retirement plan needs to address.

Many people are in denial, but things like this happen to a large percentage of us. It is important to recognize that doctors now are capable of helping us through major health-related problems that were previously lethal, thus we are living longer.

It is critical to identify how you will pay for long-term care. In the event it is needed, there are only three ways to pay for it:

1. You can self-insure, which means you pay for it yourself.
2. You can transfer risk to an insurance company.
3. You can use a special type of trust to shelter your assets so that you qualify for Medicaid earlier.

Basically, (1) you pay, (2) an insurance company pays, or (3) the state pays, or you can use any combination of the three. There is no right or wrong answer here. It depends on your circumstances, what you value, the size of your retirement portfolio, etc. There are many factors that go into this decision, and each retiree will have a different set of financial and health-related circumstances that will need to be evaluated.

First, you need to determine the value of your assets, and to what degree you may need to transition the costs away from you. Generally speaking, if you have an investment portfolio greater than $1 million, self-insurance becomes a viable option. However, if you have less than that amount, transferring risk or having the state pick up the cost starts to make more sense. There are a number of ways this financial risk can be covered, as you will find out in the next two chapters.

No two retirees are ever the same, and therefore, no two retirement financial plans are identical. Knowing the options available may be the difference between retiring well and dying without a penny to pass along to your children or grandchildren.

CHAPTER 15

How Insurance Companies Help You Transfer Risk

If you're in a position where you're considering transferring some of the risk of long-term care to an insurance company, you can choose from three different paths. They don't need to be stand-alone plans; they can be combined.

1. Traditional long-term care insurance
2. Using annuities with long-term care riders
3. Using life insurance with long-term care riders

TRADITIONAL LONG-TERM CARE INSURANCE

A number of years ago, as medicine evolved, the idea of long-term care was becoming an issue. Whenever there is a health concern, insurance companies develop a plan to help protect people as well as make money. In the 1980s, when insurance companies started creating long-term care insurance plans, there were no standards.

When the 1990s rolled around, the market had matured and developed some basic standards. Soon, the government got onboard. The government thought it was a good idea for people to buy long-term care insurance because they knew that if someone doesn't have insurance or money to pay these medical bills, the state would have to pick up the tab.

Together, our government—along with the insurance industry—created what is called *tax-qualified long-term care insurance.* If an insurance company created a long-term care insurance plan that met certain criteria, the government would partner with them and give consumers tax benefits for buying these types of plans. One could deduct a certain percentage of their premiums, and the benefits would be considered tax-free. In essence, the government incentivized individuals to buy the plans, as long as the insurance companies maintained certain standards.

As soon as the government got on board, the insurance industry decided that almost every policy they created would follow those guidelines. Thus, long-term care insurance became popular. Fast forward to today, there are many people who've been paying these premiums for years. They have now reached the stage requiring care, and they're collecting benefits. Insurance companies have realized that the benefits they promised to pay are much larger than ever anticipated because the cost of healthcare has skyrocketed.

Insurance companies are losing money on these policies in large amounts. It has gotten so bad that now, it is almost impossible to find an insurance company that will write traditional long-term care insurance coverage. In addition, the companies that did write policies in the past are trying to get out of the business. To get out of the business, they have to do one of two things, (a) sell the business to another insurance company who's willing to buy it, or (b) get rid of all the policyholders in whatever manner possible. Increasing policy premiums is one method that's commonly used.

The problem is no other insurance company wants to be in that business either because they know they're going to lose money. They cannot find another company to buy this block of business away from them unless they essentially give it away, creating a big loss.

Therefore, the long-term care insurers start to steadily increase premiums until almost everyone has dropped their policies and the company can exit cleanly out of that business. That's the route many of these companies are choosing. What about the poor policy owners? They have been faithfully paying their premiums for many years. Suddenly, they get a notice in the mail, for example, that says, "Dear Mr. and Mrs. Smith. In the long-term care industry, the expenses are greater than we anticipated. As a result, we're going to have to increase your premiums by 170 percent: 60 percent this year, 60 percent next year, and 50 percent the third year."

Your options as a policyholder are (a) accept these premium increases, (b) drop the policy, and the company really hopes you're going to pick this one, or (c) reduce the benefits of your policy. Typically, when that last option is offered to reduce benefits, they're structuring that reduction to limit their risk and price the risk more appropriately. You've faithfully paid this company for years, and now they increase premiums so much you can no longer afford the coverage. You are forced to drop your policy right before you need it.

To recap, the challenges with traditional long-term care insurance are essentially:

1. Almost no companies are in this business anymore.
2. If you do find a company, the premiums are high and they will only get more expensive.
3. To get the coverage you have to be very healthy, and it

is the most difficult policy to get approved. It is easier to get life insurance than it is long-term care.

As a result, fewer and fewer policies for long-term care coverage are issued every year. It wouldn't be surprising if, five or ten years from now, this type of insurance were to become a footnote in history.

Let's discuss the second way insurance companies can help you transfer risk.

USING ANNUITIES WITH LONG-TERM CARE RIDERS

People either seem to have positive or negative thoughts about the word *annuities*. The financial press tends to focus on the negative, saying that annuities are expensive and tie up your money. This may be true for some types of annuities, but not all. There are many types of annuities available, and the media is good at highlighting certain areas without giving you the whole story.

As we age, it's natural to want to put money in safer types of financial instruments. In the annuity world, there are tools called *fixed-indexed annuities* that protect principal and offer the opportunity to get a decent rate of return. This is the annuity space with an overwhelming majority of long-term care *riders*.

These long-term care riders are typically linked to something called an *income rider.* To best illustrate this, let's give an example of the way an actual insurance company works as of this writing.

Imagine you want some of your money structured in such a way to generate income on part of your portfolio. Say you have $500,000 saved for your retirement, and you think it's a good idea to take a portion of that portfolio and use it to generate an extra $1,000 a month of supplemental income. Depending on your age, you could place $200,000 to $250,000 in one of these fixed-indexed annuities and get a rider that would guarantee that you could withdraw $12,000 a year for as long as you live.

In most states, if you need any type of long-term care, an annuity like this would give you the option to double that payment to $2,000 a month or $24,000 a year, usually for a maximum of five years. This length of time can vary. This certainly is not enough money to pay for long-term care; rather, it is additional funds you didn't have before. For someone getting $2,000 or $3,000 a month, to have that income double to $4,000 or $6,000 a month can start to make a pretty decent dent in those medical bills.

The other option with these types of annuities is to invest the money more conservatively, but only if you don't need the income today. The longer you let it accumulate, the higher the amount of income, and thus the higher the amount of long-term care benefit.

PROS

The advantages with these types of annuity plans are that if you're not taking income, the benefit grows over time. They tend to be inexpensive, with long-term care riders typically at 1 percent or less. Other benefits are that you don't need to be insurable, you can use annuities as an alternate strategy to bonds, and you can use IRA dollars.

This last advantage, using IRA money, is a big deal because this is one of the few ways you can access those dollars for long-term care benefits other than self-pay. In addition, if you're taking distributions for long-term care, normally the write-off for the healthcare need is large enough that it offsets the distribution, so it ends up being a tax-free distribution.

Let's expand on "annuities can be used as bond alternatives." Many people looking for bond alternatives in their portfolios find that annuities fit nicely. With today's interest rates so low, *investment-grade bonds* are paying little, as low as 2 percent or 3 percent. These types of annuities are paying similar rates, although some pay as much as 6 percent a year. If you can get an annuity that earns 3 percent to 6 percent a year, in today's low interest rate environment, that alone is a reason to hold this annuity. If the annuity also happens to have long-term care benefits with potential income benefits attached, *sometimes for free*, the choice becomes clear.

If you want half your money in stocks and half in bonds, putting a sizable chunk of the half that you want in bonds into this type of annuity makes sense. It's a great way to make your money multitask with the same dollars, performing multiple functions.

CONS

The disadvantages to annuities with long-term care riders are that the benefits are often limited, and some offer less coverage in early stages and more coverage later in life.

Typically, these plans are not enough to cover the whole cost of care. The annuities with income riders and long-term care riders are generally designed to supplement long-term care, as opposed to paying for all of it. In addition, you may have to wait ten to fifteen years for the benefits to accrue. Of course, this is assuming that you're not taking income with these funds, but letting them grow instead.

It's important to note that if you need long-term care two years from now, the long-term care benefits with this type of annuity are not going to be large. Let's say you're seventy years old today, but you aren't going to need care until you're in your eighties. Because there's time for these benefits to accumulate, they could potentially deliver a significant percentage of the future costs of your healthcare.

USING LIFE INSURANCE WITH LONG-TERM CARE RIDERS

A third way to transfer risk is by using life insurance with long-term care riders. This area has experienced recent growth and interest from both clients and insurance companies. Insurance companies have been writing life insurance contracts for years. They know how to price that risk; it's easy when combining life insurance policies with long-term care. They are essentially selling a *guaranteed lifetime death benefit*, which are typically *guaranteed universal life contracts*. This means your premiums are identified at the beginning; they're level and they're guaranteed to stay at that rate every year for life.

In addition, the death benefit is also known and is guaranteed. If the death benefit is $1 million, that number will not change. As long as you pay your premiums, you get the death benefit; it's that simple. The long-term care benefit is really nothing more than an acceleration of the death benefit, which means you can start receiving payments earlier while you're alive, provided it's used for long-term care.

The triggers to qualify are normally *two out of six activities of daily living,* which are eating, bathing, dressing, toileting, transferring, and continence. If you need help with two out of those six activities, then you're approved to draw some of your death benefit funds for long-term care. If you're incapacitated mentally with Alzheimer's, dementia, or other conditions, you also have the right to receive these benefits.

Whatever portions you do not access for long-term care are paid out to your beneficiaries when you die. For instance, if you have a $1 million life insurance policy with a long-term care rider and spend $300,000 to pay for that care while living, there will be approximately $700,000 left over that will go to your family after you're gone.

PROS

The reason clients like this type of insurance is that there are no unknowns in these plans. The premiums with traditional long-term care policies increase over time, and you never know how much they'll go up each year. You also don't know if the benefits will be available when the time comes. Their premiums might get so high that you'll have to reduce your benefits in the future or drop the policy altogether. It's murky territory, whereas with a life insurance contract with a long-term care rider, everything is known. You know what your premium's going to be every single year, as well as your death and long-term care benefits. It's a huge advantage for you when there are no surprises.

Further, you can choose various payment methods. You could pay a certain amount every year for your lifetime, every ten years at a time, or in one big lump sum payment. The insurance companies are flexible with structuring payments in a fashion that works for you.

Another strong reason to buy this type of insurance is that the death benefit is large and you have access to a lot of benefits right away. If you start one of these plans and either die or become disabled within a few years, it becomes the best investment you've ever made in your life. It's an attractive option for many people these days.

CONS

First, you have to be insurable. You don't have to be an Olympic athlete, but you must be in relative good health. As mentioned earlier in the book, conditions like diabetes and heart problems can exclude you from coverage.

Second, there's a lot of benefit earlier in the life of the

insurance contract, and a little less down the road. Even while the death and long-term care benefits remain the same, as the cost of care increases over time, the benefit becomes worth less because it does not keep pace with inflation or the increasing costs of care. The same dollar amounts that seem appropriate today may not cover as much of the care you will need later in life.

The third disadvantage to life insurance policies with long-term care riders is that you cannot use IRA dollars to buy them. *You can only fund life insurance with after-tax dollars.* If the vast majority of your money lives in pre-tax accounts like IRAs, 401(k)s, and 403(b)s, you must take a distribution to get this type of coverage. You'll have to pay tax on that distribution and make sure you've pulled enough out to have after-tax money left over to pay the premiums. This isn't necessarily bad, but you cannot hold these types of life insurance policies inside the IRA—you will have to move money out of your IRA first in order to buy them.

LIFE INSURANCE—EVERYBODY WINS

One of the biggest benefits of life insurance is that the insured always gets back more money than what they pay. Even if someone never needs long-term care and lives to 100 years old, the death benefit is paid out to a family member. The insured party will never pay as much money in premiums as the death benefit they receive.

Alternatively, if you need long-term care, you will get that money as well as the residual death benefit left over. If you need that care early in the term of the policy, you make a lot of money. If you need it later, you still make a good amount, but either way, *you are guaranteed to make money with the life insurance approach.* It always equals more money than you'll ever put in. From an investment standpoint, it always makes sense.

I know what you're thinking: how can life insurance companies stay in business if they pay the people more in benefits then they charge in premiums? I can assure you, the life insurance company will also make money. They are not in this business just for the fun it.

Say you're sixty years old and pay an insurance premium of $10,000 a year to get $500,000 of life insurance. What if you live to 100 years old? A $10,000 a year premium paid for forty years is $400,000. If your death or long-term care benefit or some combination thereof is $500,000, someone is your family is guaranteed to make money. Over forty years, that benefit may average out to only a 2 percent rate of return. Meanwhile, the insurance company has had your money for forty years, and all along, they've been investing it wisely and making 6 percent or more.

On the other hand, let's say you're sixty years old when you start this insurance program and you've only paid premiums for ten years. When you turn seventy, you suffer a stroke or you die. You've paid $100,000 in premiums, but your family gets $500,000, which is about an 18 percent annualized rate of return.

Life insurance programs represent a declining rate of return the longer you live, while annuities represent an increasing rate of return the longer you live. If you combine the two, it's an effective way to maintain a growing benefit base for your long-term care needs.

If you're young and can get traditional care, it might be beneficial because you can get a lot of coverage for little money. If your premium is doubled in the future, it's doubled from such a low starting point that it's worth paying the extra expenses. It's still inexpensive and worth considering if you're younger than sixty years old.

Many people assume they are not insurable, or that long-term care insurance and life insurance will be too expensive at their age. Most often, they are incorrect on both counts. Unless they've had a heart attack in the last year, have diabetes and need insulin, or are currently battling cancer, more people are insurable today than ever before.

In addition, it is a false belief that insurance is cost-prohibitive at sixty-five or seventy years of age. Because people are living longer today, thus paying premiums for a longer period of time, someone buying life insurance today at age seventy is essentially paying the same rate that they paid twenty years ago at the age of fifty. That's how much insurance premiums have been reduced over time.

HOW DO YOU KNOW WHICH OPTION IS BEST FOR YOU?

When it comes to transferring risk to insurance companies, the answer is always my lawyer's favorite, "It depends." While there are many factors that weigh on this decision, the following is an excellent planning tip that may help as you discuss long-term care strategies with your spouse and Certified Financial Planner™.

What I often recommend is to combine the life insurance approach with the annuity approach. That means you buy a smaller life insurance contract today that creates a lot of long-term care benefits early on, and then combine that with an annuity, maybe in your IRA. Over time, the annuity benefit increases. Therefore, you will have a base of life insurance long-term care benefits while the annuity benefit drops on top, increasing every year to help keep pace with inflation. A combination approach like this is often quite successful. Something of this nature is not a strategy you should try to plan yourself;

you will need to seek out professional help in crafting the right plan.

The bottom line is if you are in your sixties with extra cash lying around in the bank, life insurance might be an attractive option. At the same time, if you have a lot of money sitting in retirement plans—IRAs, 401(k)s, 403(b)s—the properly structured annuities are fantastic.

I want to close this chapter with an extremely important point—*make sure you're working with a fiduciary when evaluating annuities*, especially those that have long-term care benefits. It is paramount to be careful in this environment as not all plans are the same, and some have real disadvantages. You want to be certain you are working with someone who is truly focused on what is best for *you*.

CHAPTER 16

Medicaid Planning

In this chapter, we'll discuss Medicaid planning; however, it's important to note that Medicaid planning will vary from state to state. Also know that it is vitally important that you *enlist the services of an elder law care attorney* who deeply understands this part of the legal code. This is a point I cannot stress strongly enough.

WHAT IS MEDICAID PLANNING?

Medicaid planning is essentially structuring your affairs in a manner so that the government believes you are out of money, or to put it bluntly, broke. If you need long-term care, they will pay for it on day one, provided your finances are planned correctly.

Because this is Medicaid, we're essentially discussing the welfare system. Medicaid only pays for skilled nursing facilities, sometimes also referred to as a nursing home. They also won't pay for a private room, only semi-private, which means you get a roomie. If you want to receive care at home, this is not going to work for you. They will also not pay for care at an assisted living facility. (Please note that Medicaid rules will vary to some degree from State to State. This is one of many reasons to enlist the services of an elder law care attorney.)

I want you to imagine for the moment that over your lifetime, you have done everything right, and you live next door to "Bob." You and Bob had the same job, worked together your entire career for the same employer, at the same location, and were paid the same amount of money. You both got married and had two children at exactly the same age. Your children went to the same schools, and you both drove the same cars.

In many respects, you were similar, but your lives diverged. You did everything right with your money. You lived within your means, contributed to the company 401(k), and saved money over the years. However, Bob did not. He never saved a dime. In fact, he spent everything he earned and then some, so he's accumulated big credit card debts. You, however, pay your credit cards off every month because you live within your means.

As you grow older, you both retire. You fortunately have

saved some money for your retirement because all along you've done what you were supposed to do. Bob, however, is scrimping by on Social Security. He has no other money. Suddenly, you and Bob have a stroke on the same day and need to be admitted to a nursing home. Remember, Bob has done nothing right financially his entire life. He's done everything wrong, and because he's done everything wrong, he is rewarded.

The state enters the picture and says, "All right, Bob. You don't have any money because you've done everything wrong. We will pay for your care starting on day one." Meanwhile, you are receiving the exact same care as Bob, but the state says to you, "Oh, no. You have money because you did everything right. You need to pay for your own care until you run out of money. Then we'll pick up the bill."

Many people would say that's not fair. You and Bob both paid the same amount of tax into the system for the same amount of time. How is it that Bob did everything wrong, yet he gets benefits from day one? You did everything right and now you will to wait several years to get any benefits because you first have to spend down all of your savings.

The goal of Medicaid planning is to structure your affairs so that the government views you and Bob as financially equivalent when the time comes.

As you can see, Medicaid planning is slightly controversial. There are a number of people that aren't comfortable with this idea. If you feel you saved enough money to be self-sufficient and not burden the state, you can ignore this chapter. There are others who look at this idea and think it sounds a bit unsavory. If you believe the state should cover the costs of care for those who can't afford it, and that those who can should pay for themselves, there's nothing wrong with that opinion. This chapter does not apply to your situation.

However, if your moral position is that it's a sneaky way for someone who can afford care to get a free ride, then guess what? That's exactly what it is. It is a legal way for people who can afford their care to not pay it. Viewed another way, it is a perfectly legal method for people to take money they would have spent on care and, instead, pass it along to surviving spouses, children, grandchildren, etc.

There are those who are uncomfortable with this concept. However, our job as Financial Advisors is to remain as neutral as possible and not make moral judgments. If it is legal and it is our client's goal, then it is our fiduciary responsibility to let them know that it is an option. That's what we'll talk about in this chapter.

Oftentimes, we see this type of planning come into play when we come across a child who is a trustee of their parent's money. Let's say the dad has passed and the mom now has Alzheimer's and has to go into a nursing home. That child is the trustee of their trust and the costs of mom's care are quickly depleting the accounts. As trustee, it is their legal responsibility to look at all ways to protect the assets of that trust or the beneficiaries, which would be the child's siblings.

If all opportunities are not explored thoroughly, the other beneficiaries of the trust have the right to sue. That trustee may be forced to look at planning like this in order to protect assets for future generations, even if they find it morally reprehensible. Mom and Dad may have even verbally said, "This money is to take care of us, and whatever is left over, is left over."

Hiring a good elder care attorney that's qualified is critical with this type of planning. They can also help shed additional light on the pros and the cons in your state.

HOW TO STRUCTURE MEDICAID PLANNING

The first step is to create a *special planning trust*. Different attorneys call them different names, but at the core, you need to create a type of *irrevocable trust*. Irrevocable means that you cannot change the terms of the trust. Once you've established this trust and put money or assets into it, you can't change anything. You are officially giving up control of your money.

PROS

Medicaid planning is essentially protecting your assets for family members. People would rather have their surviving spouse or children spend that money than give it to a nursing home. Many people would rather anyone get the money. They view nursing homes like they view the IRS. And I have yet to meet anyone who was happy with giving their money to the IRS.

CONS

The number one disadvantage is that you will be in a nursing home. You won't be living at home, which is where you may want to be. You also won't be in assisted living, which is likely your next choice. You're going to end up in the last place you probably want to be: a nursing home.

In most states, in order to protect an IRA, 401(k), or a 403(b), you need to first cash them out, pay all the tax, then take the remaining after-tax balance and put it into these trusts to protect them. That's often the only way to protect an IRA.

Another option is to annuitize the IRAs. This means you must take the income. There are special rules how to do this. You cannot take it for longer than life expectancy as defined by the Health and Human Services Department of that state. This is an area where you've really got to enlist the help of that elder care attorney.

This is also an expensive area because of its complexity. The attorney has to possess specialized knowledge, and it is not surprising to see attorney fees in the tens of thousands of dollars. It could be $20,000 or more for an attorney to execute this type of planning. At the same time, if that attorney saved you $500,000 in spend down—meaning they protect $500,000 for your family—then a $20,000 or $30,000 bill doesn't seem so large.

With this type of planning, you're typically putting money into irrevocable trusts using various methods. The challenge with this is acknowledging that with an irrevocable trust, you're essentially giving the money away to the trust. It's designated solely for the benefit of your children and grandchildren. You cannot use it as an income generator to buy a car or take a cruise. That money is gone, as far as you are concerned.

However, a number of attorneys might name a child or other family member as a trustee. That trustee could make a distribution on behalf of the beneficiaries, and the money might somehow magically find its way back to Mom or Dad. This happens all the time. But if the state finds out, it collapses that trust, and now all that money is available for the Medicaid spend down. This is a strategy you should avoid.

These trusts with this type of planning are most appropriate for people who know there are portions of their portfolios they will never need. They know it's going to their children regardless. If this is the case for you, then these tools are more attractive.

Remember, in this specialized area, one tiny mistake can lead to colossal problems. In an ideal world, you want an elder care attorney who also is knowledgeable about *special needs trusts*, because these trusts are similar. Both types of trusts are designed to take advantage of the benefits the state provides while keeping assets out of the state's hands.

I know many people who worked with an attorney who said they could prepare this type of plan, only to have the state laugh at them and say, "You can't do that." Those attorneys did not know what they were doing, but thought they did. Many states have special classes and licensing to qualify as a *certified elder care attorney*. That's what you need to look for when hiring an attorney.

HOW CAN YOU SHELTER ASSETS FROM THE MEDICAID SPEND DOWN?

Every state has its rules when it comes to Medicaid spend down. Generally speaking, the rules are as follows: before the state will pay for your care, you must verify that (1) you own no more than one home with equity of less than

$500,000, (2) you own one car, and (3) you have less than $2,000 to your name. The $2,000 is divided between *countable assets* and *non-countable assets*. Countable assets are essentially everything in your name—your investment account, your bank account, and for most states, your retirement account.

Interestingly, some states say that if you're over the age of seventy and a half, your retirement accounts are non-countable. However, your required minimum distribution is countable. If you are married, they often have a spousal allowance. Your spouse can keep a certain amount of non-countable money in his or her name. Say this amount is $100,000. States differ, but imagine your spouse has an IRA of $500,000. They spend $400,000 of it on your care, then they could have $100,000 left in their name.

With life insurance cash values, you can only have perhaps $1,000 of cash value; however, a large area of non-countable assets are *Medicaid-qualified annuities*. These are essentially annuities that pay out all of the money, similar to a pension annuity, on a schedule that is a period of time shorter than the life expectancy of the person in the nursing home.

The reason these are attractive is if you're in a nursing home, you will probably not live to life expectancy. If your life expectancy is ten years and you only live to three, your surviving spouse and children get the remaining seven payments. These special irrevocable trusts are non-countable assets. If it's in a *living trust*, which most people have, that is considered as a countable asset. This game of qualifying for Medicaid is basically transitioning assets from the countable column to the non-countable column.

An odd scenario with Medicaid planning is that sometimes it makes financial sense to divorce your spouse if they go into a nursing home. I know this sounds crazy, but the way the system is set up, by divorcing your spouse, you are no longer liable for their debts. They may then be able to qualify for Medicaid benefits more easily, while you can protect more of your assets from the spend down.

Obviously, this is completely backwards from any normal thinking, but it does come up.

You do want to watch out for slick salespeople when it comes to Medicaid Planning. There are people out there giving seminars to try to convince you that this area requires a lot of pre-planning for something that might occur ten or fifteen years out. The reality is that most of this planning doesn't need to occur until you know that someone's going to need some type of care in the next few years.

In fact, a lot of planning can be done in what's called *crisis mode.* For example, someone has a stroke and now they need to move to a nursing home. This usually happens within a short period of time. Almost all this planning can be done when you are trying to get qualified for a nursing home. Don't be sold on the concept that you have to plan ahead, at least not under current law. Beware of the slick sales person who tries to get you to do all this "advanced planning." It is rarely necessary and usually nothing more than a way for them to get paid for something you don't need right now.

If you learn nothing more from this chapter than my next statement, I will have succeeded:

It is an absolute must that you hire a qualified and certified elder care attorney to properly execute this type of planning.

There are Financial Advisors who tell you where to invest your money to protect it. They say that when the time comes, they will get an elder care attorney involved. The truth is, if that attorney is not involved at the beginning, then you're being sold something.

Medicaid is a state program, but the federal government manages a big portion. Because they're spending money hand over fist, states are becoming quite aggressive when collecting the money they're paying out in Medicaid. In some states, you can protect your house. Other states will say you can only protect the house as long as you're living in it. However, the minute you move out, you will need to sell it, and they will collect the money from the sale. The house will then belong to the state.

Because Medicaid is administered on a state-by-state basis, it's hard to offer general rules. Every state has its own idiosyncrasies. Because of this, again, I need to tell you it is an absolute must that you hire a qualified and certified elder care attorney to properly execute this type of planning.

SECTION IV

Estate / Legacy Plan

CHAPTER 17

Estate Planning 101

Most people nearing retirement haven't looked at their wills and trusts for twenty to thirty years. This is normal. We don't wake up in the morning, look at our spouse lovingly and say, "Honey, let's get our wills and trusts updated today."

Retirement often generates a signal in people's minds to update important documents. We find these documents tend to be out-of-date—in some cases, pretty significantly.

Please be aware as you read this section that I am not a practicing attorney. Although I collaborate with them regularly regarding specific estate laws where my clients live, it is critical to consult with a qualified *estate planning attorney*.

KNOW THE DIFFERENCE BETWEEN WILLS AND TRUSTS

The objective of wills and trusts is to transfer all assets to someone else when you pass away, as quickly and efficiently as possible. These assets might include property like real estate, cars, motorcycles, boats, recreational vehicles, jewelry, diamonds, works of art, or even personal items such as clothing, etc. In many cases, these assets may include any number of different financial accounts.

Wills and trusts are similar types of documents, but the differences can be dramatic. You also need to understand *powers of attorney*—what they are, what they do, how they are the same and also quite different. This helps determine the best route to transfer assets from your name into someone else's name.

YOUR WILL IS A PUBLIC DOCUMENT

A *will* is simply a set of instructions written to the *probate court*. If you have a will in place when you die, your assets go through a process called *probate*. This process varies with each state. In some states, probate is a pretty simple and easy process. In other states (California and Florida to name a couple), probate can be time-intensive and costly.

When you die, the judge of a probate court is given your will to review. That will name someone as your executor or personal representative, depending on your state.

This person is responsible for distributing your assets, essentially moving them from your name over to other people's names, by following the instructions you have set out in the will. Even though you've spelled this all out in black and white on paper, everything must still be approved by the court.

For many people, this is a perfectly acceptable procedure. If most of your money is in financial accounts, and if you set up your estate properly, the only asset going through probate, in this case, would be your home. Keep in mind that if you're married, everything goes to your spouse, and that's a simple process. But it can get more complicated, as you will see.

Because the decisions of the probate court are public record, whenever your assets are transferred, if one of your children or beneficiaries is not happy about how things are being distributed, all they have to do is raise their hand and say, "I object." They hire a lawyer and before you know it, all your beneficiaries have to hire their own lawyers, resulting in a good old-fashioned *will fight*. Attorneys love these types of battles because they are usually the only team who wins in such a fight. It can get messy and public, often taking years to resolve. This is something that we want to avoid.

If you only own a home and some personal belongings

outside of your financial accounts, a will is a reasonable method to handle your affairs. Assuming your financial accounts are set up properly, you can get a will drawn up by an attorney inexpensively—typically, for less than $1,000. You can also visit websites such as LegalZoom.com and they will walk you through putting together a simple will.

USE A TRUST TO AVOID A COURT BATTLE

The number one reason people use a *trust* is to accomplish the exact same goals as a will; however, they want to bypass probate court and avoid the probate process.

A trust also performs better than a will at providing control after death. For example, let's assume you have three children. Two of those children have done well in life. They are model citizens and make smart decisions with money. They're the kind of children that we all dream of having. Then you have one kid, little "Johnny," who is not good with money. If he gets a lump sum, you know darn well that it's going to be spent before he even receives the money. Instead of giving out the money all at once, you want to spread it out over time. A trust is going to be a more appropriate tool to accomplish this. In addition, if you have children with special needs who might receive benefits from Medicaid, a trust would be an appropriate legal document to use for that type of beneficiary. Anytime you want to restrict distributions or control from the grave, as they call it, you might use a trust.

HOW DO YOU KNOW WHICH TO USE?

I use a checklist in my practice to help decide which path is likely more appropriate. If you can answer "yes" to any of these items below, you may want to use a trust.

1. Property in Multiple States

If you have property in multiple states, you want to have a trust. Otherwise, your children will have to go through probate in each state you own property in, which will require multiple attorneys and get extremely expensive. A trust avoids all of that.

2. You Are in a Second, Third, or Fourth Marriage

There can be a lot of children in this scenario, and a trust is effective for anyone outside of a nuclear family—meaning one husband, one wife, and 2.3 children—as it delineates exactly who gets what and avoids the court fights that can erupt when children from numerous marriages all want a piece of what you are leaving behind as you pass on.

3. You Want to Control Money from the Grave

You don't want to pay out all the money at once as previously discussed. That's a good reason to get a trust.

4. Half of Marriages End in Divorce and You Want to Be Cautious

You want to make sure that after you're gone, your assets go to your children and not your ex-in-laws. You want to protect those assets for your child or grandchild.

5. You Want Privacy

You don't want your estate listed in the public record. It may be worth paying extra money to have a trust completed and avoid probate, which becomes public record.

6. You Have Significant Assets

People with significant assets may end up facing estate taxes after they die. If you have a sizeable estate, depending on what the estate tax laws are both federally and in your state, you may want to utilize trust planning to reduce those taxes.

There are other examples, but those are the basic reasons to choose a trust over a will.

Please understand that there are a number of assets that

don't go through wills or trusts at all unless you've given a specific directive. Primarily, these are financial assets, such as retirement and insurance accounts. We're going to talk about how to best handle those in the next chapter.

FUND THE TRUST

When a trust is created, you have to *fund the trust*, which simply means *retitling your assets* into the name of the trust. Let's say if John and Mary Smith have a joint bank account that is not included in the trust, it doesn't matter what the trust dictates. In order to fix this, you would go to the bank and retitle that bank account into the name of the trust—for example, "The John and Mary Smith Family Trust." The same is true with property or real estate. Anything you want to go through the trust has to be titled in the name of the trust. This is how the trust gets funded.

If you have a trust when you die, anything that has been titled in the name of the trust is controlled by the trust. If any of your financial accounts are either (a) titled in the name of the trust, or (b) have the trust named as beneficiary, then those accounts are controlled by the trust.

However, what if you don't get everything transferred into the name of the trust? Perhaps you bought a piece of property and you forgot to put it in the trust. Typically, whenever there's a trust, there is also what's called a *pour-*

over will. This document states that anything you forgot to put in the trust goes into the trust after you die. The only problem with this is that it is still a will, meaning those are instructions for the probate court. All those assets that you didn't put in the trust have to go through probate to get into the trust; and remember, the reason to use a trust in the first place was to avoid probate.

Many states are trying to make it easier to avoid the probate process without going through the expense of a trust. For example, a house is really difficult to transfer from your name to another person's name short of doing a *quick claim deed* or putting it into a trust; therefore, it is hard to avoid probate. To resolve this, many states are setting forth laws to make it easier for people to transfer their home to their children or other beneficiaries after they're gone. Every state is different, so hiring a qualified *estate planning attorney* will help you follow the rules. The good news is it tends to be inexpensive because it's a fairly standard practice for an attorney.

POWERS OF ATTORNEY

In addition to wills and trusts, there are other documents you will need with estate planning, and those are primarily called *powers of attorney*. First of all, you have what is called *durable power of attorney*. This is simply a document between a husband and wife allowing the husband to sign for the wife, and the wife to sign for the husband. Essentially, the purpose of a durable power of attorney is to help make decisions if one person is incapacitated.

For example, the husband has a stroke and lives in a nursing home. The wife still has to file a tax return with the husband's signature, but he can't physically sign because of his stroke. A durable power of attorney allows the wife to sign his name on his behalf. This applies to making any decisions on financial or legal accounts. If she wants to sell the house, for example, she can sign on his behalf. That's a durable power of attorney.

There are also *healthcare powers of attorney,* also known as *medical powers of attorney*, depending on your state. Healthcare or medical powers of attorney are similar documents allowing you to sign on behalf of another person for medical decisions. For example, should you pull the plug in an end of life situation? There are also *living wills* that lay out your instructions for this question. There can also be a variety of directives in a living will, such as "do not resuscitate."

The purpose of these documents is primarily to help people make decisions on your behalf. Typically, a husband and wife would hold power of attorney for each other. However, if one dies while the other is still alive, or if one gets Alzheimer's and now they're both in a nursing home, a second level would be named who would have to exercise those powers. Typically, this is a child.

Sometimes, you may want one child have the responsibility of the financial decisions (durable power of attorney), and another one could handle the medical powers. Sometimes it's the same child and sometimes it's not even a child, but a friend. *The point is to have these documents in place* so someone can make decisions for you when you are incapable. If there are no powers of attorney in place, then someone must request a type of *guardianship* or a *conservatorship* over you from the court. This is a difficult issue that takes time to resolve with the courts, and is extremely costly.

Don't be "penny-wise and pound-foolish," by doing it yourself regarding wills and trusts. If you make a mistake in your estate planning, no one will discover it until you're dead, and by then, it's too late to do anything about it. You've left behind a huge mess and your family ends up paying more money for attorneys than if you had involved an attorney from the beginning.

Always look for an estate planning attorney because there are plenty of attorneys who "specialize" in just about everything. If you ever see an attorney advertising, "We specialize in personal injury, workmen's compensation, divorce planning, family planning, estate law, etc.," walk away. This is not specialization. You want to hire someone who lives and breathes estate planning, day in and day out, and nothing else.

WHAT HAPPENS IF YOU DIE WITHOUT A WILL OR TRUST?

If you die without a will or a trust, your assets still go through probate, but now there's no will to give the probate court instructions pertaining to your assets. This is called *dying intestate*. Every state has its own rules for this.

Let's say you are married with four children and live in the state of Texas. When you die without a will or a trust, the state dictates that your spouse gets the community property, which is basically your house plus one-third of your personal property. The children inherit everything else.

If you have an IRA with no beneficiaries and you don't have a will or a trust, the estate becomes the beneficiary. Your spouse gets one-third and the kids get two-thirds.

What if you have no children but you have a spouse and your parents are living? In this scenario, your spouse gets community property, half of your separate real estate, and the parents get everything else. Neither of these are probably outcomes you anticipated.

Let's compare this with Michigan. In Michigan, the spouse gets the first $150,000, plus half the balance. The children get everything that's left. It gets increasingly complicated with second and third marriages and multiple children having different parents.

It's pretty rare that these intestate rules would ever represent how you would actually split up your inheritance after you're gone. If you're curious, type "intestate laws by (your state)" into Google and see what comes up.

The bottom line is to make sure you get a will or a trust in place to avoid these unwanted scenarios. If you don't have a will or a trust, the state will provide one for you, which is most likely *not* what you want. A slog through probate court is something you should try to avoid entirely.

CHAPTER 18

Financial Assets

In the last chapter, we mentioned that financial accounts—when wills and trusts are structured properly—could avoid probate. The reason is they tend to transfer through a process known as *contract law*. Let's explore the various types of financial accounts, the general categories, and how they transfer from your name into someone else's name, efficiently and effectively.

HOW FINANCIAL ASSETS GO THROUGH THE ESTATE PROCESS

We'll begin with retirement accounts. These include IRAs, 401(k)s, 403(b)s, 457s, simple IRAs, SEP IRAs, Roth IRAs, profit-sharing plans, etc. There are many others, but they all share one commonality: when preparing a retirement plan, you must identify the primary and secondary beneficiaries.

If you don't remember ever setting up a beneficiary, you might not have. With every one of these accounts, there is a default beneficiary called your *estate*. If you don't name a person, charity or a church, then your estate becomes your beneficiary. Essentially, if your estate is a beneficiary, that account will be cashed out, taxes paid, and pushed through the probate process that we mentioned in the previous chapter. Therefore, *it is exceedingly important to name beneficiaries.*

With most retirement accounts, if you're married, your spouse is your primary beneficiary. However, your spouse does not have to be. You can name anyone else as a primary beneficiary, but typically, you will need your spouse's signed approval.

Beneficiary arrangements trump or supersede everything, including your will and/or trust.

Your will might say that your 401(k) goes to your three children, but your 401(k) beneficiary arrangement says it goes to your second or third wife. When you die, it doesn't matter what your will says. It doesn't matter what your trust says. It doesn't even matter what a divorce decree says. That money goes to the beneficiary listed on the account paperwork. Period.

On the plus side, you can change this every day if you wish; it is as easy as signing your name to a new beneficiary form.

WHAT ACCOUNTS ALLOW FOR DIRECT NAMING OF BENEFICIARIES?

All retirement plans allow you to list beneficiaries. All insurance contracts, which include life insurance, annuities, etc., also allow beneficiaries.

Many times, a married couple will visit our office, and we find out this is not their first marriage. When I ask them to provide a list of the beneficiaries on their retirement and insurance accounts, they realize they haven't changed them in years. Sometimes, a husband in his third marriage discovers his beneficiary on his $300,000 life insurance policy is still his first wife. If he had died and we hadn't caught that error, where would the money have gone? Wife number one, because she is listed as the beneficiary.

I'll share a true story of one of my clients who was divorced and remarried. "Janet" had one child from her previous marriage, and her ex-husband, "Bill," never remarried. His will and trust dictated that his 401(k) would go to their only child, a daughter. However, he never changed the paperwork on his 401(k), which listed his ex-wife (my client, Janet) as the beneficiary. When he died, Janet got the money.

To make matters worse, there was no *contingent beneficiary* listed. If he had listed his daughter as the contingent beneficiary, Janet could have said, "I will disclaim that."

This means she could step aside and let the account go to the next level of beneficiaries, in this case, her daughter. The problem was there were no next-level beneficiaries. In order to give the money to her daughter, she had to cash out the account.

It gets worse. Janet was remarried to a highly successful businessman, which put them in the 40 percent tax bracket. Therefore, when she cashed out the 401(k), almost half the money went to the IRS and state income taxes. As a result, their poor daughter was left with half the money in that account because Bill failed to change his beneficiary on his 401(k).

How would this have been different had he simply added the daughter as a contingent beneficiary?

If he had, Janet could have "disclaimed" the account as mentioned earlier, and it would have then gone to the daughter. The daughter would have had the opportunity to "stretch" that 401(k) over her lifetime. In other words, she could have taken out a small amount of money each year via a required minimum distribution schedule. This approach would allow her to accept that money over many years, thus stretching out the benefit, leading to reduced taxation.

Thousands of dollars went to the IRS that could have been

avoided, all because Bill did not understand the power of beneficiary arrangements.

This happens all the time!

People make this mistake all the time because they don't realize that contracts like retirement and insurance accounts with named beneficiaries overrule all other documents. There are only two ways these accounts would *not* pay out to a named beneficiary: (1) the beneficiary is in jail, or (2) the beneficiary is the reason that the account needs to be paid out. In other words, that beneficiary was complicit in the murder of the contract owner or account holder. Sounds like an episode of *Law & Order*, but I've seen it happen.

The naming of beneficiaries on these accounts is a far more powerful tool than people understand. It is extremely important to review them regularly, as it is quite easy and common to make life-altering mistakes.

OTHER TYPES OF ACCOUNTS

There are other types of financial assets that do not offer beneficiaries. For example, you could have an *after-tax brokerage account* in your joint name. When one person dies, it goes to the joint owner (normally a spouse). What happens after the second person dies?

Historically, that account would go through probate. One of the reasons for a trust is to handle accounts like this. Instead of holding the account in a joint name, you would create a trust and place it in the name of the trust.

However, there is zero reason nowadays to pay to have a trust created for that type of account. There is now a registration called *transfer on death (TOD)*. Every brokerage firm or custodian I know uses a TOD form, which is nothing more than a beneficiary form for after-tax investment accounts.

For example, let's say you have an account at a major brokerage and sold a property or recently inherited money you want to invest. If you ask them for a TOD form, they will happily hand it over. This form designates who gets the money and how it's distributed after you're gone. It's essentially a beneficiary form. You sign the form and, if you die, that money goes straight to the named beneficiaries.

Why doesn't that major brokerage firm automatically ask you who you want listed on your TOD form when you initially set up your account? The answer is simple. When those forms are utilized, after you die, the money goes to your beneficiaries immediately. The beneficiary can move it to his or her Financial Advisor, spend it, or whatever they want. The odds of that money staying at the initial brokerage holding the account are low.

Alternatively, if you haven't filled out that form, your assets have to experience probate before they go to the beneficiary. This could be as long as six months and up to two years of time that the brokerage firm gets to hang onto your money. They can make money on your investments while your account is tied up in the probate process. Because it benefits them, it is not in their best interest to offer you these types of tools.

This is a great opportunity for you to determine to what degree your financial institution and advisors are truly focused on what's best for you. If you have after-tax accounts and this is the first you've ever heard of a TOD form, that should tell you loud and clear your current advisors/brokerage firm aren't interested in what's best for you. On the other hand, if you already have signed TOD forms, set up because your advisor or institution is on top of this, then you can feel confident that, at a minimum, they are paying attention to your best interests, insofar as beneficiary arrangements are concerned.

Bank accounts are the last category. As previously stated, state governments are trying to make avoiding probate easier. However, the only financial accounts that have yet to offer TOD forms are bank accounts. My understanding today is that every state has a similar account tool called *payable on death (POD)*. No one really knows why the banking industry wanted their own terminology, but the

POD at a bank is essentially the same as a TOD form from a brokerage; they both accomplish the same outcome of naming beneficiaries.

So, in review, there are *beneficiary arrangements* for life insurance and retirement accounts; transfer on death (TOD) forms for after-tax investment accounts; and payable on death (POD) tools for bank accounts. They all mean the same thing: how to quickly and efficiently transfer assets from your name to the name(s) of the people you designate in the event of your death. And again, these documents all supersede wills, trusts, and divorce decrees.

AN EASIER WAY

One simple trick to make your life easier, especially for people who have a trust, is to name a spouse as primary beneficiary (if you are married) and a trust as secondary beneficiary on everything you own, where a beneficiary can be named. That way your spouse controls the assets when you die. When he or she passes, your assets will go through the trust. If the trust is beneficiary of everything after you and your spouse are gone, that trust can efficiently distribute assets in the manner you see fit. Therefore, if you want to make changes to beneficiaries, you don't have to worry about changing them across your multiple accounts—you only have to change them in the trust, which is now your *ultimate beneficiary*. This is much more convenient and a simple way to avoid mistakes. We will discuss the most common of these mistakes in the next chapter.

CHAPTER 19

Common Mistakes

This chapter will review the top five mistakes people make with their estate planning. Each of them are easily avoided.

1. DOCUMENTS NOT UPDATED

The biggest mistake by a large majority is failure to update documents. When I meet with a couple or an individual for the first time, it is extremely common for them not to recall the last time they had their wills and trusts updated. The only time I get an answer is if they recently retired, because when someone retires, that becomes a trigger point to update their planning. Otherwise, they typically haven't looked at this for twenty or thirty years.

Another thing I hear is "time flies." Many clients think they've updated their documents within the last few years when, in reality, ten or twenty years have passed. In that time, things change. I ask for a copy of everything before I put together a comprehensive retirement plan.

When reviewing documents with a couple I recently worked with, they told me that they updated their estate planning documents three years ago. When they brought their documents into the office, we learned that it was twelve years ago, not three. Since their last update, grandchildren had been born, they sold their house, and none of this made it into their trust. Their estate planning documents had not been updated to reflect those major life changes.

My recommendation is to review your estate planning documents or have them reviewed every five years at a minimum, plus whenever a significant life event occurs. It might be a new child or grandchild, a new home, or when someone gets ill or dies.

2. BENEFICIARY BLUNDERS WITH FINANCIAL ACCOUNTS AND ASSETS

Updating any of your accounts with named beneficiaries is really important. Assets with out-of-date beneficiaries that still list your old spouse, for example, can wreak havoc. I'll illustrate the possible consequences with a few examples.

Two couples I worked with made the exact same mistake

and we caught the error; however, different outcomes would have occurred because of some unusual rules with retirement accounts. In both cases, the husband had started a retirement plan before they met their wives. As a result, they didn't know whom to name as beneficiary back then, so they both did what many people do and named their parents as beneficiaries. They both got married, had children over the years, and were now preparing for retirement. What I'm about to tell you is almost mind-boggling, but it happens a lot.

This is the point where I met each of these men. I asked for their beneficiary statements and found that, surprisingly, they each had worked at the same company forever. Neither of them ever changed the beneficiary of their retirement accounts. In both cases, their parents had passed away. They never thought about the fact that their named beneficiaries might not be living.

Thankfully, we caught this mistake and corrected it in time. However, consider the scenario where these two families had never met someone like me who, at the very least, looked into these documents. Many Financial Advisors ignore beneficiary arrangements because they don't get paid to do that.

Here's what would've happened. The first gentleman, we'll call him "Jack," had his money in a 401(k). Interestingly, if Jack died, his 401(k) would automatically pay out the benefits to his wife, Barbara, regardless of who is listed as beneficiary.

A little-known rule with 401(k) plans is that if you are married, your spouse is your default beneficiary. Even if Jack's parents are still alive when he dies, and they are listed as the beneficiary, Barbara would still get the money.

401(k) plans assume that a living spouse is intended to be the 100 percent beneficiary. The only way to get around that is to have that spouse sign a beneficiary form that gives up those rights.

Our second husband, we'll call him "Charlie," was a teacher. He didn't have a 401(k); he had a 403(b). In almost every way, these two accounts work identically; however, if Charlie died, that money would follow the beneficiary tree first, starting with his parents if they were alive. Because there was no living beneficiary, if he died, the money would have gone to his estate to be distributed via intestate rules. These rules follow whatever the probate rules would have been on his estate. Therefore, the money may or may not have gone to his wife.

In other words, 401(k)s and 403(b)s function similarly, but have a few different rules. There's a famous story in New York about a man with a 403(b). Before he met his wife, he named his parents first as beneficiaries and his sister second, and he never updated the beneficiaries. He died with over a million dollars in his 403(b). His parents had already passed on. His wife was expecting the money, but it did not go to his wife. Instead, it went to his living sister who hated his wife. This man's wife of thirty years got nothing. These are terrible mistakes that can happen with retirement accounts if you are not careful.

Every week, I see people with old life insurance contracts where the beneficiary is someone other than their current spouse—an old spouse, a parent, a friend, a brother or sister. This is so important, because if your beneficiaries are not correct and current, money goes to strange places and not where you want.

The irony is changing a beneficiary is the easiest thing in the world. All you have to do is get a simple beneficiary form. With compliance and regulations, they might be up to four pages these days, but typically, they're one or two pages. All you do is write down the beneficiary update, sign it, and you're done! The beneficiaries have been changed. You have the right to change your beneficiary any time you feel like it—every day if you so desire. The problem is not that it's difficult; it's that nobody remembers to do it.

3. BENEFICIARY BLUNDERS WITH CHILDREN

I have three specific examples to share regarding this topic.

There is a case about an older, divorced gentleman with three sons. He named his sons as beneficiaries of his $600,000 401(k) account. When he died, he wanted each of his three sons to get one-third, which is roughly $200,000 each. So far, so good.

However, he meets bride number three and is married to her for about a month, at which time the excitement of being married to a new bride apparently gives him a heart attack and he dies.

Who gets the 401(k) money?

One might assume the three boys because they are the named beneficiaries, but this is incorrect, as we learned a few paragraphs ago. If this were an IRA, 403(b), or almost any other account, it would have gone to the boys. However, because it's a 401(k), the payout goes to the new spouse of thirty days. The boys sued, got crushed in court, and lost. This case actually made it all the way to the Supreme Court. They still got nothing.

My second example pertains to something called *per stirpes*. This phrase is what 99 percent of people would want to use on their beneficiary arrangements if they understood what it meant.

Let's say you have three children—Johnny, Suzie, and Baby Jane. Johnny has three children, Suzie has two, and Baby Jane has none. You list your beneficiary as your spouse first, and after you're both gone, you want everything split equally between all three of your children. What if one of those children dies before you do?

If you do not have this per stirpes verbiage, here's what typically happens: the money gets split *per capita*, which means, if Baby Jane dies before you, she has no children, so her share would then split 50/50 between Johnny and Suzie. This seems fair.

However, if Johnny dies first and you don't have per stirpes listed, then those grandchildren get disinherited. Per stirpes means "through the bloodline." If you don't have this in place, Johnny's share gets split between Suzie and Baby Jane. Essentially, you have unintentionally disinherited three of your grandchildren.

I actually stumbled across my third example the other day, and it's a simple one. You welcome a new child into your life, but forget to add them on your beneficiary list. I had a couple that had two boys, who were now grown. One of the boys already had their own children. This couple adopted a little baby girl when they were in their fifties. They forgot to add that little baby girl as a beneficiary on their accounts. If they had died, the two adult boys would have split the assets 50/50, leaving their beautiful baby girl with nothing.

My clients were stunned at this news. They assumed all their children would equally split their inheritance. I informed them that because they instructed everything to be split evenly between the two sons in their documents, that is exactly what would have happen, regardless of the new child. That's an example of a life event where planning did not get updated.

4. NOT FUNDING TRUSTS

This is another estate planning mistake we see *all* the time. To create a trust, you go to the attorney's office, spend time figuring out how all your assets will be distributed. You do all this planning to avoid probate. You finally receive your trust documents in this impressive, gigantic three-inch thick binder that's packed with hundreds of pages. You breathe a sigh of relief. Congratulations, the trust is written, but you are only 90 percent of the way to completion.

Herein lies the problem. All of those papers mean nothing unless you actually fund the trust, which means *titling assets in the trust.* You would retitle your home, bank accounts, and after-tax investment accounts into the trust. It could mean making your retirement accounts or life insurance the beneficiaries of that trust account you just created. The point is that you actually need to finish the job.

If you don't follow through with the other 10 percent of this job, then that trust is basically worthless. It's worthless to you because when you die, nothing will be in the trust. Thank goodness, your attorney wrote a *pour-over will,* because everything that's not in the trust will then go into the trust. That is what the pour-over will dictates, but what does that mean? This means that everything will go through probate.

Again, why did you write the trust? To avoid probate. You paid the attorney all that money for what is essentially nothing if the trust is not funded.

I had a single mom come to our office the other day. She had eight rental units and not one was titled in the trust. That meant every one of them would go through probate. If she had died without correcting this, that would have been a nightmare for her children.

It is essential that you remember to fund your trust. Your attorney will tell you what steps to take to fund the trust once it's been established. The problem is you have to do it, and it's challenging to find the time when you are so busy. You have to go through every account you own with every financial person you work with and retitle everything. You have to go to the county and the deeds department to retitle your house and property. It's a pain, and many people "forget" to finish these extra but most critical final steps.

You could have the attorney do it for you, but understand they will charge twice as much to manage funding your trust. If setting up a will and trust package costs $4,000, it might cost you a total of $8,000 just to complete that last step. However, the good news is if you go this route, you avoid the hassle and can feel confident that it's done properly.

5. NOT PROPERLY INTEGRATING FINANCIAL ACCOUNTS OF THE ESTATE PLANNING DOCUMENTS

A big misconception is that your will and trust dictate who will receive your inheritance and how. Say you want your son, Bobby, to get your IRA and your daughter, Suzy, to get the life insurance pay out. As discussed previously, in reality, the will and the trust have zero impact on where that money actually goes. It goes to the beneficiaries listed in the IRA or life insurance policy.

When creating your estate plan, your attorney will instruct

you to retitle your IRA with Bobby as your beneficiary. However, the second line, or contingent beneficiary, needs to be changed into the name of the trust. You will have to consult with your Financial Advisor to make this change. Then you have to go to your 401(k) and make the same change. Your life insurance also needs to be changed, and so on.

Your attorney is attempting to get everything running through the trust, in order to whittle it down to one master document after you're gone. This way, if you make changes in the future, there's only one document you must change.

A few weeks ago, a client came to me explaining he and his wife followed through and retitled everything in the previous four years. They went to the banks and changed all the names, they retitled their house, changed names on their after-tax accounts, and changed the beneficiaries on their IRAs and 401(k)s. About two years ago, they got a new financial advisor. That new advisor opened up new IRAs. They moved the 401(k), but the new advisor did not retitle the beneficiaries properly. He named each spouse as beneficiary and did not name a second contingent beneficiary.

In fact, on one of the accounts, instead of naming the trust as the beneficiary, he actually named the children as direct beneficiaries. This couple, who thought they had all their ducks in a row, were dumbfounded. They did not find out until they came to us for a second opinion and I discovered the error when reviewing their documents.

The big financial institutions do not get paid to make sure beneficiary arrangements are an accurate reflection of the client's wishes. If your Financial Advisor is not pointing this out to you on a regular basis, it is so easy for the documents to become outdated. Everything gets jumbled, and goofy things happen with your money after you die. Don't make that mistake. Make sure everything is coordinated.

Every year in January, we send a list to our clients asking them to confirm the accuracy of their beneficiaries. In addition, with every face-to-face meeting, we review their portfolios and again bring it to their attention. It becomes ad nauseam, but "better safe than sorry."

Conclusion

FINDING AN ADVISOR

In conclusion, it is important to understand that in most cases, when you consult a Financial Advisor, you're actually talking to an investment consultant who focuses solely on investing. This is not good or bad, but you need to recognize that is all they do. Their primary job is to build a portfolio.

They will talk to you about asset allocation and, typically, will focus on getting the best returns possible. There is a marked contrast between what that person does and what a *wealth manager* does. A wealth manager goes far beyond investment consulting. They also handle tax planning, meaning they will not only review your tax returns, but they also might do them for you and help reduce those taxes, today and in the future.

A wealth manager will also help with insurance planning. They will look at your life insurance planning, long-term care planning, and even your healthcare insurance. They're going to help you identify the best path to take with regard to overall estate planning.

They will also assist with your income planning, particularly in retirement. From which accounts will you pull income? How will you structure those accounts to generate income? How do you optimize your Social Security benefits to make your money last? These are all questions for your wealth manager, who typically can do a lot more for you than an investment counselor.

When you're working, an investment counselor might be the only thing you need. All you're trying to do at that stage of your life is grow your portfolio. Once you are nearing retirement, however, working with a wealth manager or a firm that offers comprehensive wealth management becomes exceedingly important.

It is not that uncommon to find people who end up failing in their retirement planning because they're only working with an investment consultant. While that person might be doing good work trying to get the best returns, they may be ignoring the risks. These retirees might get caught with a tax liability they never expected, or even lose everything to future healthcare expenses because no one was advising them on their entire retirement plan. You want someone bringing all of these areas to your attention in retirement; sometimes, these are areas you never would have considered.

ASK THE RIGHT QUESTIONS

How do you know that you're talking to someone who is right for you when it comes to your retirement? There are a few questions you need to address that should give you the answers you seek.

TELL ME ABOUT THE SERVICES YOU PROVIDE YOUR CLIENTS.

Preparing tax returns and providing tax planning in retirement should be near the top of this list. *Tax planning in retirement is a big deal.* You want to make sure you're working with someone who's comfortable with those discussions and helps their clients plan in this critical area.

If their services revolve only around investing your money, this is probably not the right person. However, if investing your money is only part of the plan they present to you and they will also help with your income planning, Social Security planning, tax planning, healthcare planning, estate planning, insurance planning, etc., and are licensed to do so, then this is a good sign that you've found someone who can help you retire well.

ARE THERE ANY TYPES OF INVESTMENTS OR TOOLS THEY DON'T UTILIZE FOR THEIR CLIENTS?

You want to be careful working with someone who doesn't use certain investment tools. For example, if someone says they don't use options or futures, you have to ask why. There are firms that claim they are a *fee-only firm*, and as a result, don't sell any commissionable products like life insurance or annuities. This is someone to avoid because annuities or life insurance might make sense for a portion of your money. That firm is not going to make those recommendations. They're going to recommend that you put your money in something that doesn't work as well for your circumstances. You want someone who is willing and able to provide all financial tools available on your behalf.

WHAT TYPES OF CLIENTS DO YOU SERVE?

If you are nearing or in retirement, the answer should be, "We only help people who are retired or nearing retirement. That's all we do." You don't want someone to say they serve high net worth investors of over a million dollars. They might have a twenty-four-year-old client who just made it rich with a tech company. Those types of people are facing different circumstances than you if you're retired. You want to work with someone who only helps people at your stage of life, because your needs are different.

CAN YOU GIVE ME REFERRALS OF EXISTING CLIENTS?

This is an excellent question because their answer will tell you whether or not they're truly a *fiduciary*. If they are willing to give you referrals, this tells you two things: (1) they are not a fiduciary, because a fiduciary technically cannot provide client references; and, far more importantly, (2) it's obvious that they don't value the privacy of their clients.

In today's world, fiduciaries have a requirement to respect the privacy of their clients, similar to the confidentiality shared with a doctor or lawyer. The same holds true in the financial world. However, what if they're not a fiduciary and are nothing more than a financial salesperson? Then they can legally give you references. So beware of the advisor willing to give you references, because *they are not an advisor that you ever want to work with*.

Imagine you're nearing retirement and trying to decide whether you can and/or should retire. You visit with a Financial Advisor and are basically handing over everything you've worked for your entire life. You are entrusting them with the nest egg you've built for twenty to forty years.

Their job is to invest that money in a manner suited to your best interests. When you talk to this potential Financial Advisor, and you're considering giving that person your entire life savings to manage, isn't it fair to assume that advisor is going to make recommendations that are in your best interest, with no conflicts of interest?

In other words, you want to be sure they will give you recommendations that you would make for yourself, if only you had the expertise. This is exactly what a fiduciary does.

For example, let's say a Financial Advisor gives you the choice to invest in two different mutual funds. Both funds are basically the same, but one is a little better for you by providing a higher potential gain, while the second fund being offered will make more money for the advisor.

If your advisor is a fiduciary, they will want to put your money in the first mutual fund because it's better for *you*. Unfortunately, the overwhelming majority of Financial Advisors out there today fall into category two. In other words, they don't have a *fiduciary responsibility*. Rather, they have something called a *suitability responsibility*. A Financial Advisor that falls under that level doesn't have to do what's best for you. They only have to make recommendations that are "okay" for you. In other words, it is perfectly acceptable for them to make recommendations in such a way that they get paid the most money.

HOW DO YOU KNOW THE DIFFERENCE?

How do you know if you're talking to a true fiduciary who puts your needs first? Here's an easy place to start: if the advisor you're talking to works with a huge national brokerage firm, the odds are high that they are not the kind of advisor you need managing your retirement planning. This is because—like I have said before in this book—they do not work for you, they work for the name on the door.

For example, if your advisor works for one of the larger national brokerage firms, or one with franchise offices at the local strip mall, their primary job is to make as much money for the company they work for as possible. The client's needs are secondary. If you want to find a fiduciary, you almost certainly have to find an independent firm that is not associated with any of these big-name companies. However, just because they're an independent firm does not mean that they are a fiduciary.

FINDING A FIDUCIARY

Be certain that any advisor you are considering is part of a *registered investment advisory firm*. If that person uses the phrase *registered investment advisor,* generally speaking, they will have a fiduciary responsibility.

To truly be a fiduciary and focus on what's best for you, they need to be licensed to handle everything, whether it's stocks, bonds, mutual funds, or insurance types of tools. This is a must, because if they aren't, then they can't truly hold themselves accountable. They're not a full fiduciary.

The biggest challenge is that there is no place you can go to search for an authentic fiduciary. The big financial firms, who are typically not fiduciaries, overwhelmingly control the financial industry. They don't want it to be easy. They would prefer to have you believe that they are making recommendations that are in your best interests, when they're actually not. Therefore, they most certainly don't want to make it easy for you to determine whether or not someone is an authentic fiduciary.

There's been some recent legislation you may have heard about. The Department of Labor is trying to mandate that if you're making recommendations for someone's retirement accounts, then you must be a fiduciary or act in a fiduciary capacity. This has been delayed, and at this stage, it is questionable as to whether or not this will become a reality. It is unfortunate that identifying a true fiduciary is one of the most challenging things for the average person to do, because there is no certification.

Being a fiduciary is a mindset more than anything else. In the financial industry, you can go out and become a registered investment advisor. By law, a registered investment advisor is supposed to act in a fiduciary capacity, but do they? They might argue that they do, but the majority of them are not licensed to do anything with insurance companies. As a result, they're basically making recommendations, but they don't have the full set of tools available to make *proper* recommendations.

Just because an advisor claims to be a fiduciary, doesn't mean they are. The two most important questions when seeking a fiduciary are, "Are you a wealth management firm?" and, "What tools do you use or not use?" If they are a wealth manager and if they use all the tools available, both insurance and brokerage, they are most likely acting as a true fiduciary.

Another question to consider is, "How are you compensated?" Many articles on this subject suggest that fees are better than commissions. However, if you want a true fiduciary, the best answer is, "We receive compensation in both fees and commissions, depending on the work we perform for each client." That tells you they do have access to all the tools out there, because some tools only compensate via a fee and some only with a commission.

Compensation should be transparent. You don't want

hidden fees. Investment advisors and investment counselors live in a world riddled with hidden fees. If you don't see any fees on your financial statement, you're most likely working with an investment counselor, not a fiduciary, and certainly not a wealth manager.

Wealth managers acting as a fiduciary, generally speaking, are open and transparent with fees. Their fees are listed on your statements, and they'll be comfortable discussing them with you. You want your advisor to be open about their compensation, and there is nothing wrong with paying them for the work they do. Nobody works for free, but if the fees are hidden, there's a reason they're hidden. Usually, it's because it's a number large enough that they don't want you to know what it's for.

Another great observation in your first meeting is to note where their focus lies. Is it your portfolio? Did they ask you to bring your statements to the first meeting? Do they immediately look at the statements and offer solutions to optimize your money management and get a better return? Are they focused on your goals? These are all questions to be considered.

For example, in our office, we spend thirty to forty-five minutes with a new client discussing their goals and what they want to accomplish before we ever look at their statements. That's the sign of a good wealth manger that is a fiduciary—they are more interested in your goals.

In addition, will that Financial Advisor you are considering using for your retirement planning be doing a *probability analysis* to identify the likelihood that you have enough resources to meet your goals? Using these kinds of analysis tools is a good thing; however, be on the lookout for a red flag.

Many advisors using a probability analysis are assuming that markets are going to average 10 percent plus over the next thirty years. This is unrealistic. Anything can look good if you're going to average 10 percent a year forever! The analysis has most likely been programmed to look artificially positive. To meet your goals for your retirement, you want the average returns used in the probability analysis to be closer to 5 percent to 6 percent. If it's anything more than that, they're giving you false hope. This is manipulation, and you don't want to be working with someone like that.

Before hiring a prospective Financial Advisor, always check them out with the Better Business Bureau. This is a great resource. If they've had complaints, you can bet it will have been reported here. You can also search on Broker Check through FINRA (https://brokercheck.finra. org/). You can look up someone's name and see if they've had complaints in the past. Both of these resources are available to the public.

Sometimes you will find that a potential Financial Advisor has had complaints. Before crossing that person off your list, let's explore a few complaint scenarios.

Imagine you looked up a Financial Advisor and found no complaints. That's great, but if you work with a company that does much business at all, there are going to be complaints. A successful company could have one thousand or more clients, and you can bet the farm that there's at least one or two difficult clients among them, no matter how good the firm is.

On the other hand, if you do find a complaint, that doesn't necessarily make them a bad company. They might have been in business for thirty years. Things happen over time, often through no fault of their own, yet people complain. The way these systems are set up, if there's a complaint, it remains there forever. If you see two or three complaints, this is not a big deal. Read them and read the responses so you can get a feel for what happened.

The complaint could have been minor in nature. For example, the Financial Advisor might have put the client's money in an investment tool that the client decided later they didn't like. The client complained and was refunded all their money plus earnings. This type of complaint should not concern you at all. The client ended up better off than when they started.

However, what if someone complained that a Financial Advisor invested their retirement savings in some crazy risky asset and they lost half their money—which is completely inappropriate for people in retirement. This is a complaint to be more concerned about. You should question if this is a habit for that advisor, or if they have learned from these past mistakes. There is nothing wrong with bringing it to the attention of that advisor and having an open and honest discussion. Get their side of the story.

What if you see a dozen complaints? In this case, I don't care how many clients they serve. That's more than there should be, and this is probably someone to avoid. Where there's smoke, there's fire.

A final word: always be on the lookout for the old adage, "If it sounds too good to be true, it probably is." For example, ten-year treasury bonds are currently paying 2 percent, maybe 3 percent by the time you read this book. If someone approaches you and says, "We can get 4 percent or 5 percent, with guaranteed accounts," this sounds reasonable. However, if someone promises they can get 8 percent to 12 percent returns with minimal risk, this is too good to be true. When interest rates are paying 2 percent and they're offering some wild number approaching 12 percent, you can be assured there is risk involved. The Financial Advisor who downplays the risk or is not transparent, is one to avoid.

RETIRING WELL

I hope that throughout this book, you have been taking mental notes, thinking about how your retirement plan is structured now and considering what changes you should be making as you enter your retirement years. This can be a glorious phase of life, full of adventure and good times, all of which can come to a screeching halt if your money runs out. Prepare now by making that critical shift to a retiring well plan, and then go out and enjoy your life in whatever form it takes.

I would be honored to come along on that ride with you.

Acknowledgments

This book would never have been possible without the input over the years of my friends and colleagues. Special thanks go out to the incredible people at Advisors Excel. Cody, David, and Derek, you three have put together an incredible team! Larry Flynn, Jon Torbet, and Art Canfield, your thoughts about how we can best help our clients have created a huge chunk of material for this book.

And of course, to all of my very good Financial Advisor friends throughout the country. I cannot possibly list all your names, but know that you have made an enormous impact on my life. I cannot express my gratitude for all of your thoughts as we mastermind together.

Most importantly, I have to thank my family for supporting me throughout. Becky, Sara, Taylor, Brendan, Morgan, and Madison. You make every day a treasure.

About the Author

 **MICHAEL REESE** is the president and founding principal of Centennial Wealth Advisors LLC. In his twenty-plus years in the financial industry, he's trained more than a thousand Financial Advisors in retirement-planning strategies. He is a Certified Financial Planner™, Chartered Financial Consultant, Chartered Life Underwriter, and Certified Tax Specialist. As the host of a television show called *Retiring Well*, he's become one of America's most recognized retirement-planning professionals. Michael's previous book, *The Big Retirement Lie: Why Traditional Retirement Planning Benefits the IRS More Than You*, has received enthusiastic reviews from readers.

You can reach out to Michael at www.cenadvisors.com, or by calling (512) 265-5000.